She Just Wanted to Dance Again

She Just Wanted to Dance Again

My Journey to Parenting My Parent
and
A Simplified Guide to Becoming a Parent's
Caregiver

CHERYL JENKINS

iUniverse, Inc.
New York   Bloomington

iUniverse books may be ordered through booksellers or by contacting:

iUniverse
1663 Liberty Drive
Bloomington, IN 47403
www.iuniverse.com
1-800-Authors (1-800-288-4677)

Because of the dynamic nature of the Internet, any Web addresses or links contained in this book may have changed since publication and may no longer be valid. The views expressed in this work are solely those of the author and do not necessarily reflect the views of the publisher, and the publisher hereby disclaims any responsibility for them.

ISBN: 978-1-4401-0775-7 (sc)
ISBN: 978-1-4401-0774-0 (ebook)

Library of Congress Control Number: 2009928890

Printed in the United States of America

iUniverse rev. date: 6/3/2009

Dedication

It was the summer of 2004, and after all these years, I found myself truly in love for the first time. We had been inseparable for over a year, and at age fifty-one, I had new life infused into me. Little did I know the strength and depth of that love would be put to the test so profoundly and so early in our relationship—but it was, and I am so blessed to have such a wonderful man in my life. This book is dedicated to Larry, my soul mate and life partner. Without his support, compassion, love, and understanding, I'm not sure how I would have survived what I've gone through over the last several years. He is my sanity and stability. He has my devotion, loyalty, and love through eternity.

Contents

Acknowledgments

Listening and offering encouragement when someone is experiencing a challenge or crisis are both valued and appreciated. Family and friends so often provide the initial strength for overcoming adversity and finding inner peace. It's important to understand and acknowledge the value of that support.

I find myself, many times, out of the blue, looking at Larry and saying, "Thank you." When he asks why, I say, "For being you." He responds, "I couldn't be me if you weren't you. Who else would I be?" We smile and continue with whatever we are doing. Larry, thank you for being you.

Mary, you are a remarkable woman. Your previous personal experiences dealing with the sometime disjointed elder care in our society is commendable. I admire you as the mother, wife, sister and sister-in-law, daughter, and friend that you are. Unknowingly you gave me inspiration when I doubted myself. You are a gentle spirit, yet a true warrior.

Becky, thank you for listening and for being there by my side when the chips were down. You are a true friend.

Christian, my son, thank you for growing up and allowing me to learn that you truly listened to all that I tried to teach you during your childhood. It really does make a difference to know that my child loves and appreciates me and that the trials and tribulations of my child-rearing experience ultimately made a difference—even though the journey included many side trips! I never stopped believing in you, and I'm proud because you have finally learned to believe in yourself.

My aunts, cousins, and other family members, thank you for listening and for your support when I felt that my whole world had fallen apart. *Family* is such a powerful word, and although through the years our lives have taken us in different directions, the connection we maintain in our hearts and our minds helps to ground us through all our experiences.

To my extended family, thank you so much for accepting me as an integral part of your family. I am honored, and I cherish your love and friendship.

Introduction

We all experience the reality of aging. Suddenly it happens, sometimes with the excruciating impact of a blow with a two-by-four. You find yourself needing to parent your parents. They were there, guiding you on the path to adulthood through minor or major challenges. Even if your parent-child relationship was rocky, there is still a connection. And now you find yourself in disbelief—the roles are doing a flip-flop.

Whatever your relationship may have been, you begin to experience a sense of loss. With this loss many emotions erupt: sadness, compassion, anger, resentment, fear, aggravation, and impatience, to name a few. The loss is not one-sided either. Parents and children, as well as other family members, may experience these emotions.

As scary as the shift in roles appears, someone needs to step up, take the lead, and guide the ship through the waters. This role may fall to different family members from time to time, as one's strengths may surface just as another's may falter momentarily—and that's okay. Caretaking isn't an exact science, as you will quickly learn, but it also does not need to be so overwhelming that it consumes and tears apart your daily lives and relationships.

Throughout history, societies have varied widely in their care of their elders. Today there are shifts in many cultures, due in part to the current economic climate and also through education and humanitarian understanding. Some societies revere their elders. In the

Japanese business culture, rank is based upon a person's age, and elders are respected for their wisdom and knowledge. Many other cultures also value the teachings of their elders and still strive to pass on their cultural heritage. Yet other cultures throughout the years, as inhumane as it sounds, would send them off to the woods to die. Our culture is somewhere in between. We have many elder services and organizations, but many times these bureaucracies become so tangled in red tape and legalities that utilizing those services becomes frustrating and sometimes costly. There's no such thing as a free lunch, especially these days. Many people believe the answers are assisted living and skilled care facilities, and they blindly believe that turning over their parents' care to an institution will resolve all their problems. In fact, these choices invite a whole new set of problems.

Today our society has become a nation of TV commercials expressing alternatives to "becoming a burden" on your family and so forth. Is that just a false front? When you call a responsibility a burden, does that make it so? Being a parent's caregiver in his or her later years doesn't have to be a burden. It should be a time of enjoyment, a time to pass on family knowledge and experiences; it can also be a time of emotional healing. I believe that we need to get back to the ancestral philosophy of caring for our elders—not just because they can't care for themselves, not because they are unable to afford a safe and secure environment, but because of who they are and the fact that we would not be on this earth if not for our parents.

Take the time to discuss with your parents and other immediate family members, even though it can be uncomfortable, scenarios that may play out as your parents' health declines. Try to come to agreement on the essential issues involved while you can all share in those decisions and can plan accordingly. If you are reading this and your situation has progressed beyond this stage, take a deep breath, for all is not lost. Recommendations in this book can still help you move forward, too.

As you read through Part One of my book, I hope you will surmise that I have been able to find solutions even for complex difficulties. The material in Part Two includes recommendations and tools to assist you as you embark upon the caretaking path, even as overwhelming as it may first appear. Finally, I have included some examples and forms in

Appendices A and B that I will discuss. These will be helpful should you embark upon a similar journey.

Aging is a part of life that we just have to accept, as it will happen to each and every one of us someday. There are no perfect scenarios, and we all make mistakes. But don't we want our children and others to remember us for the person we are and what we've accomplished? Let's take the time to learn from each other and pass on our knowledge, skills, and compassion to our children. Then, when they need to take care of us, they will have the practical and emotional resources to do so.

In making your way through tangled emotions, dig deep, for this can become a healing time too, as it has become for me.

Part One:

The Abbreviated Version

Chapter 1:
Life Can Flip-Flop
At Any Time

Ground Zero

It was late one afternoon during the first week of July 2004. We were anticipating a relaxing and enjoyable Fourth of July weekend. I traveled weekly for work, and Larry had retired a few years earlier. We were looking forward to my upcoming four days off. And then … the phone rang. It was a friend of my mother, telling me that she had fallen and been taken to the hospital. The doctors didn't have many details but were quite concerned, as Mom was very delirious.

On this occasion, Mom's neighbor had just left for a week's vacation. Another of Mom's friends had planned to check with her more frequently by phone. I generally called Mom several times a week and had just spoken with her the previous day. Mom, eighty years old, walked with a walker, though begrudgingly. On this particular morning, while trying to maneuver herself into her small bathroom, she lost her balance and hit the back of her head on the bathtub as she fell to the floor. Her friend had called several times, leaving messages on the recorder, and Mom hadn't responded. However, sometimes she didn't answer her phone or respond to her messages, so nothing really seemed out of the ordinary.

Three days later, hearing her other neighbor outside her house,

Mom called out for help although she hadn't spoken to this neighbor for the past thirty years. The neighbor called 911, and the paramedics had to break a second-floor window to get in. Mom had been lying there, in and out of consciousness, for more than three days. She was dehydrated and had a severe urinary tract infection. She also had several pressure wounds from lying on the floor between the tub and toilet in one position for so long. She could not pull herself up off the floor. Due to the extent of her dehydration, the doctors said she would not have survived if the neighbor had not heard her cry for help.

I had moved to Florida more than twenty-two years ago. Mom still lived in Ohio in the same house where my brother and I grew up. We moved into our house around 1959. Dad passed away in September 2001, and three years later, Mom still was refusing to move. She was still in denial regarding her own health issues. Mom's health was deteriorating, and my regular trips to Ohio were proving pointless in convincing her to make a change. Mom and Dad only had two children, my brother and me. My brother, four years younger, had passed away in October 1991. I only had one child; my son was born in 1978 and also living in Florida. He was rebellious and not too cooperative when it came to the concept of being a responsible adult. Mom's friends were aging also and not able to help much. Other family members were spread out, and her sisters too were confronting their own issues. Mom's one neighbor checked on her daily, which was a real blessing for me.

Since Dad died, I continually tried to point out the importance of Mom making certain rational decisions, as opposed to me or someone else making them for her. My pleadings fell on deaf ears, as did my wanting her to wear an emergency medical alert. Had Mom explored other options rationally and not been so stubbornly opposed to moving from her home, where she found it difficult to maneuver with a walker, she might not have experienced the severe chain of events that impaired her daily existence. Mom had experienced a number of falls over the years, some resulting in injuries such as fractures to her pelvis. Her home was not a safe place for her anymore, a reality she would not accept.

Mom and I had many discussions, some quite boisterous, on these matters. The concept of change wasn't easy for Mom to accept. It was only after hearing her physicians say she could not live alone that she let me move her to Florida. She begrudgingly acknowledged that in her present condition the move was inevitable, and that she had lost the argument. This fall and her condition really scared her.

Just as we were settling in for a relaxing Fourth of July weekend, the phone rang, I learned about my mother's latest fall, and all was turned upside down. We immediately scheduled flights out the next morning. I called the hospital to make contact and get what information I could. Because of the Privacy Act, the amount of information one can obtain is limited until authority is established. Thank goodness Mom had executed a durable power of attorney and health care surrogate after Dad passed away, and I kept these documents readily available in the event of an emergency. I'll discuss those forms in more depth in Part Two.

I missed the next thirty days of work. I decided quickly that Mom was moving to Florida. On previous occasions I had told her that if she refused to make the decision for herself and subsequently experienced a life-altering situation, I would make that decision for her. The time had come.

Over the next thirty days, Larry, my partner in life, and I made daily, sometimes twice-daily visits to the hospital, and we began sorting and packing up items in her house. Many of the items were things Mom and Dad had acquired since they were first married, or even before that! Mom was quite the pack rat and repeatedly refused to let me sort through things during my previous trips to Ohio or have yard sales to lighten the load. After my brother passed away in 1991, Mom and Dad brought many of his belongings, including clothes, furnishings, and other household items, all the way from California. With Dad's passing in 2001, Mom absolutely refused my efforts to remove any of his belongings, too.

Mom enjoyed cutting out coupons and getting refunds. She utilized my old bedroom to lay out coupons, labels, and box tops to support this interest. She also stockpiled all the items she received from the refunding there. Yes, she had quite a few Viagra clocks, Kotex Frisbees, baseball caps with various logos, and so on. Mom also loved rummage sales. She could have opened her own fully stocked resale shop and still had plenty of clothes, bedding, dishes, glassware, figurines, and other items left at home.

When pulling clothes from the many closets, trunks, dresser

drawers, and boxes, I came across Mom's red chiffon dress. When I was a child, she would only bring this dress out when going to a dance during the Christmas holidays. Mom and Dad loved to go dancing and were quite good at jitterbugging. I flashed back to images of her in the dress with her silvery spike heels, silver handbag, and the bouffant hairdo so characteristic of the fifties and sixties, and Dad in his shiny gray suit, white shirt, and red tie. I remembered how all I wanted then was to have a red chiffon dress like that one when I grew up, and to feel it flow through the air while dancing. Their night out dancing was an escape from the daily routines of work, cleaning, cooking, and raising two children on a one-income budget. It also represented carefree fun, enduring romance, independence, and some relief from the discipline of a conservative style of life. Mom being a homemaker, I'm sure she found those nights out dancing a transformation back to a simpler, less stressful time in her life.

We had to keep pushing forward. I am my mother's only surviving adult child, so the only person I could truly lean on for help was the new love of my life. Sorting through fifty-some years of memories in a few short weeks, along with the decision to move Mom, was a *huge* emotional and physical challenge, to put it mildly.

When we got to the hospital each day, Mom would greet us with nearly illegible scribbled notes of items. In panic, she'd say, "I have to take it to Florida." She would get quite upset with me when I would reject some of her requests, stating we just didn't have room to take everything. I think one of the most bizarre requests, one that I heard on more than one occasion, was to take the group of rocks from the flower bed behind the house. Persistent in her requests, she would proceed each time to tell me where each rock was from and which vacation each one represented. I finally gave in, took a box, and gathered the rocks to accompany us on the ride to Florida. Oddly enough, they still sit in a flower pot outside our home. Now, however, Mom usually doesn't remember anything about them.

We did take many of Mom's valuables and memorabilia items, which currently adorn her area in our home, to provide some familiarity in her surroundings. Her dining room set and corner cupboards presently contain her crystal, flatware, and china, which were important to her, as well as photos, certain figurines, throws, bedding, and so on.

I remember Mom getting extremely angry at me some years prior for throwing away the rubber bands that came wrapped around the newspaper. Similar arguments occurred from time to time when I tried disposing of other nonessential junk, such as older magazines, newspapers, and old, empty plastic containers. Mom had lived through the Great Depression, and frugality is very common in the people of that era. However, I've found that people of other generations also save and cling to objects. The behavior appears to be motivated by the fear of losing control or realizing that one has in fact lost control over some parts of one's own life.

The more entangled we became in the house-clearing process, the more apparent it was that the real issue was relinquishment of control rather than throwing things away. I remember Dad getting upset about her pack rat traits at one time. He said, "Throw it away, and don't let your mother see you do it." Drawing on his philosophy, I was able to minimize the arguments by simply throwing things away on the sly. I had to invoke the theory that what is out of sight is also out of mind. The stage had been set for a challenging venture.

> **"It is sometimes better to ask forgiveness later than to ask permission first." – Grace Hopper**

Chapter 2:
The Schedule

Weeks One and Two

We had one month to accomplish our plan, since I had to get back to work. Larry and I would dumpster dive behind department stores every night to find boxes, flattening them to load as many as possible into the trunk and back seat of the car. We worked room by room. I would determine what was being packed for the trip and we would store the rest for a huge yard sale we had decided to have within the next two weeks. With some of the main rooms on the first floor packed from floor to ceiling with boxes, we weren't done yet—there was the second floor and its rafter storage, the full basement, and a two-car garage with rafter storage and an extended storage area off the rear side of the garage. Remember the fifty-plus years Mom had had to fill this space, and let me reinforce once again the fact that Mom was a pack rat!

Since Mom had shown me most of her hiding places after Dad passed away, I had a good idea where to find her valuables. She kept money stashed in envelopes in unrelated files. She kept her sterling flatware in a brown grocery bag in the back of a cabinet in Dad's work room. She kept money and other valuables in a false window front in the basement and also in a cubbyhole behind a built-in cabinet drawer. There were other envelopes too, taped to the bottoms of drawers. It's vital to be thorough when recovering a parent's valuables. We knew we had to look in everything, and we did just that, which meant that we found yet more valuables. I've even heard of people hiding things in paint cans and in containers in the back of the refrigerator.

In the midst of all our packing, sometimes our only sanity came in laughter—about all the empty jars and containers, packets of sweetener or jelly, bags and bags and bags of plastic grocery bags and used bread bags, and jars and paper towel rolls with rubber bands around them. Some rubber bands were so old that they had fused together. There were shoe boxes filled with old candles. We found drawers of plastic bags with old linens, towels, and scarves, all washed, pressed and labeled as to when they were bagged up and to whom they belonged. There were empty plastic margarine containers, cans and boxes of old, outdated food, tubes and tubes of toothpaste, a multitude of toothbrushes, combs and hairbrushes. There were old medications and ointments, some dating back thirty years. There were notepads, pencils, pens, rulers, paperclips, and scrap paper, not to mention all the receipts for bills neatly organized in boxes from the last fifty-plus years. Yes—I did say *fifty-plus years*! Medical bills and utility receipts all came with pertinent personal information. I even found bills and other documents from my maternal grandmother. I had to sort through and pull any medical information and documents containing Social Security numbers and box them up to handle later, in Florida. Whew! What a mess!

I remember trading stories with my cousin. We found ourselves in tears from laughing so hard. She told me about cleaning out her parents' house when moving them from Ohio to Arizona years back and finding dozens of Miracle Whip jars. More recently, my aunt and uncle moved to Colorado Springs to be closer to my cousin, and when emptying cupboards before selling the home in Arizona, my cousin found yet more jars. My cousin figured that the original jars somehow must have multiplied.

Could some of this behavior be hereditary? Believe me, I started reflecting on my own keepsakes, and the panic began to erupt! But wait—so much of this stuff was coming to Florida with me, too. I felt a sudden, gnawing urgency to get home and begin lightening my load!

On one occasion, I remember finding envelopes stuffed in a drawer containing pre-printed address labels. I noticed that Mom, at some point after Dad died, had cut his name off each and every label—hundreds of them! The image of her doing that and the grieving and crying she must have done! Whoa! … It left me with tears flowing profusely from my eyes.

In the meantime, I scheduled an appointment with a realtor to list the house. Once again, I can't stress enough the importance of having a parent execute the documentation to allow his or her adult child to handle business affairs such as banking, bill paying, real estate transactions, etc. The house went on the market, and I assured the realtor that the house would be completely empty and clean by the end of the month. The clock was ticking.

The first two weeks went by fast, and the two-day scheduled yard sale was quickly approaching. In the meantime, we took boxes and cans of unexpired food to the local food bank and donated clothing and other items to two local churches we were affiliated with through the years. Each time representatives from the churches came to the house, they each took several vans and truckloads of items for their parishes' rummage sales. One church took some furniture to add to their common area. The days were long, and we were numb and totally exhausted—a movie scene with walking zombies comes to mind. Even so, the tears kept flowing. I must have easily lost ten pounds in water weight! (I was actually losing a fair amount of weight through sheer exhaustion rather than failure to eat.)

Family members from surrounding areas stopped by, and some helped out. But they too would become overwhelmed. Mom and Dad had many antiques, too, which I knew we had to pack up for the trip to Florida to deal with later. Even in our exhaustion, we kept pushing ahead.

Mid-July—End of the Second Week

It was time for the yard sale. We ran out of time to sort through the entire basement and had to pull aside the things we didn't mean to sell, cover them, and just pray. We blocked off the rest of the house, and Larry relentlessly continued to pack. Several friends and family members helped monitor the yard sale, including my son, who had come from Florida for a couple of days. I had helpers staged outside and inside, and I roamed from the basement, back porch, and outside, just praying we didn't lose too much in the flurry of activity. People were nice and helpful once they found out about our situation. I also saw many people I hadn't seen in years.

By late afternoon on Saturday, everything that was going to go had gone. We gave things to family members and friends who had said that they liked certain items. A neighbor arranged for a dumpster the size of a midsized moving truck to be delivered, and we completely filled that dumpster. By this time we were even giving things away to anyone who would take them. The emotional magnitude of the task was far beyond even my expectations.

Week Three

We were now focused on preparing for the trip back to Florida. We had to make the drive, staying one night on the road and unloading the truck into several storage units I had secured over the phone, and then fly back to Ohio the following morning to finish cleaning the house and finalize Mom's trip to Florida.

We secured the largest rental truck we could obtain for the drive back, which also meant we had to stop at every weigh station along the way. We hired several local high school football players to help load the truck. We spent the day packing up the truck and left that same evening. We collapsed at the hotel that night and awakened early to drive the rest of the way the following morning.

The drive to Florida had its moment of humor when we missed pulling into the agricultural weigh station inside Florida's border. We were immediately swarmed by patrol cars and flashing lights. We stopped at all the other weigh stations but figured that since we didn't have agricultural products, it didn't pertain to us. Thank God that after talking to us they didn't make us open the rear doors. We were packed so tightly that I don't think we would have been able to reclose them!

While unloading the truck the next day with the help of several hired men, we learned that the rehab and nursing facility where I planned to place Mom somehow suddenly did not have room for her. Frantically I started calling acquaintances who were professionals in the medical field for recommendations of other nearby facilities. I found one that had an opening and quickly paid them a visit, looked over the facility, and secured Mom a room. We also set up Mom's future assisted living apartment for after she was released from the rehab facility with some of her furniture from Ohio. Talk about utilizing every waking minute of the day (caffeine was our friend—whatever it took to keep our eyes open)! There were times we felt we could have literally taped our eyes open because they felt so heavy and our exhaustion was so intense.

We flew back to Ohio the next morning to continue our relentless task. I had to put in notifications of change of address, close accounts, and attend to other similar transactions. Dealing with the banks was a bit of a challenge, though not as difficult as it might have been because of actions Mom had taken earlier.

On Friday of that week, the doctors finally agreed that Mom could travel on the upcoming Monday. I was able to secure a direct flight for the two of us. Larry stayed behind to continue cleaning the house and await my return.

In addition to Mom's challenges, including the complications from her fall, was her neurologist's grim prognosis. As a result of the compressed nerve damage in her neck area, she might be paralyzed from the waist up within several months. He wanted to perform surgery. He also identified the onset of dementia. I insisted that we would address her medical situation in Florida.

Week Four

Mom was recovering slowly but was still very weak and disoriented. The doctors released her from the hospital on Monday with the understanding that we were heading straight to the airport, an hour's drive, for a nonstop flight to Florida. Mom was afraid of flying, so the doctor prescribed a mild pill to calm her prior to and during the flight. She could barely walk, so a wheelchair was a necessity. With copies of her medical records from the hospital in hand, I knew there would be many more challenges ahead. The airline provided assistance through baggage check and making our way to the gate. We flew on Southwest Airlines since they do not assign seats, which made it great for boarding passengers needing assistance early. We were able to get first-row seats.

The flight was approximately two hours long. To add to the

adventure, we landed in the middle of a thunderstorm. My son picked us up at the airport. We arrived at the rehab and nursing facility by 11:00 PM that night.

Again, two days later, I flew back to Ohio. Larry had Mom's car serviced for the trip to Florida. We finished last-minute details at the house. It was a very sobering moment for me, letting go as we drove away. I can't remember one day over that entire month that I didn't have tears in my eyes. This whole ordeal had been an emotional drain and more damaging to my health than I realized at that time. We finalized the last of our work in Ohio and left for yet another road trip back home to Florida.

The house sold within the first sixty days. I couldn't have been more relieved; autumn was approaching, and I didn't want to have to worry about possible repairs or preparations for a northern winter.

Emphasize the importance of preparing for inevitable life-changing events. Try to insist that organizing, downsizing, and other preparations be accomplished while times are less stressful. These activities can actually be very cathartic experiences.

Chapter 3:
The Nightmares Begin

The year 2004 was such a blur. Between August 13 and September 25, Florida experienced four major hurricanes: Charley and Frances, both Category 4, and Ivan and Jeanne, both Category 3. Of course we were in their paths. Putting this in perspective, Mom arrived in Florida July 26, and Hurricane Charley began assailing us around August 12, lasting several days.

We couldn't remove Mom from the facility to evacuate for the hurricanes because she would not be guaranteed a room when she returned. Other area beachside facilities were planning to evacuate their residents, and every empty bed would be filled. Larry and I lived in a smaller manufactured home at the time. Even if we combined our belongings in a larger storage unit, we could not bring her home with us. The entrance and layout there were also ill-suited to her current physical limitations. With the onset of the hurricane, we were under evacuation orders. We rode out each of the four hurricanes, along with our cat, on the floor in the lobby of the rehab and nursing facility. They were very accommodating to families of the residents, and we couldn't have asked for more. They provided food for everyone who stayed and even allowed the many family pets to take up temporary residence. There was a flurry of activity, but this was a blessing. There were children and pets everywhere, but everyone handled themselves and their pets quite well. We maneuvered a piano into the elevator, bringing it down from the second floor. We played it in the common area, singing songs with the residents and participating in other activities. This also seemed to help ease the residents' anxiety over the impending storms.

Each of the four hurricanes passed, and each time as we arrived back at our home, I was overcome by emotions and tears. Homes around us had water damage. Several across the street had become flooded from the canal behind them. Trees had fallen on roofs, and some homes had roofs ripped off; but we were spared. We had tree limbs down and a lot of brush to clean up, but our home did not sustain any damage. It was as though God had said, "Your cups are overflowing right now."

At the same time all this was happening, my own health was besieged. In December of the previous year, my immune system deteriorated and reached its saturation point. I always suffered from allergies and sensitivities to odors that bothered me with reactions ranging from headaches to actual impaired breathing. My allergies to tree nuts, peanuts, and pine were even severe enough to cause anaphylactic reactions. But this time my situation was different—much different. My system was shutting down, and nothing seemed to completely calm my shortness of breath. I had trouble focusing and at times struggled with my memory and concentration to the level that it impacted my daily activity. I sought out an environmental specialist several hundred miles from our home, and this specialist finally provided me with some hope. However, relief would require me to make tremendous modifications to my daily routine. I also developed an allergic asthmatic condition and required a nebulizer twice a day. I had to learn to administer injections twice a week to assist in controlling my pollen and dust/mold allergies. Additionally I had to work from home and completely control my environment to help support my failing immune system. I had to adhere strictly to a routine to begin minimizing my reactions as best I could. It was like living in a bubble. I've been very lucky to this day that my company supported a telework program; otherwise I would have been in a vicious cycle of missed work, medical leaves, and hospitalizations. I've been with my company for twenty-two years now. That ordeal is a whole other story.

Please imagine my situation: not only do I have Mom's medical situation to deal with, but now my own health is trying to "kick me in the ass." Did I mention that the wonderful man in my life was still around? I also had issues with my son, but we won't go there. But wait—two months after bringing Mom to Florida and in the midst of four hurricanes within several months, I was diagnosed with type I diabetes. I became totally insulin-dependent and had to give myself between six and eight shots of insulin per day and test my blood sugars every two hours. Then, thirty days later, I was hospitalized. At first the doctors thought I'd had a stroke, but my problem turned out to be Bell's palsy, which had been brought on by the diabetes. Already taking two allergy injections per week, I had to add the multiple daily insulin injections and learn the eating restrictions to treat my diabetes. I was a pin cushion and a basket case! (Presently I use an insulin pump, which has simplified my routines and enabled better control of my diabetes.) Bring it on—try to kick me when I'm down, will you! Can you even begin to picture the chaos? And the doctors wanted me to reduce the stress in my life drastically … yeah, right!

As I know each family's situation is different, I truly understand how blessed I am to enjoy the ongoing support I've had. Dealing with elderly parents is not easy, but just remember that most of them will be the first to admit that their lives, too, are not easy.

In the following weeks and months, we would go to the rehab facility at least daily to see Mom and take her out to dinner and shopping sometimes. We tried to keep the daily contact to help ease her anxiety and confusion about the move to Florida. Our visits also reinforced family participation and promoted daily contact with the staff at the facility.

Despite the depth of several of the pressure wounds, the staff anticipated that Mom would need to stay at the facility only several weeks. Remember, we could not accommodate her at home and needed to rely on the facility's accommodations. We had to gather and do her laundry daily due to the drainage from the wounds. We took her to weekly and biweekly doctors' appointments for the next six months, the majority of them with a local osteopathic chiropractor to begin reversing some of the damage to her neck area from the fall.

However, her stay at this facility extended into a six-month stint. We had an assisted living apartment reserved and furnished with her belongings, waiting to accommodate her. However, after several months of hearing that it would be "probably another week" before she was released, only to be sent back the following day, we soon gave up hope; we relinquished the apartment and moved her furnishings back to storage.

Florida's regulations require a pressure wound to be healed to a stage two wound before an assisted living facility may admit a resident. Mom's pressure wound was still a stage four, pushing five. The wound specialists' failure to agree on the status of her wound meant she had to move back to the rehab facility. Then we began taking her as an outpatient several days a week to an outside wound specialist for more aggressive treatment of the wound.

At the same time, I was literally blind from my high blood glucose levels, having just been diagnosed with diabetes. The doctor said that my vision would clear in about eight to ten weeks, but my condition was scary. Again I relied on Larry, who drove both Mom and me to our doctors' appointments.

We became part of the furniture at the facility, and the nurses and administration knew us on a first-name basis. That familiarity helped tremendously, especially when Mom would have an issue. And there were issues! Being in the rehab section, Mom would continually get new roommates. Some were fine, while others annoyed her, and she would then rudely demand to be moved. Still I tried to be understanding. After all, can you imagine living the last fifty years of your life with your family, in your own home, free to come and go and do pretty much as you please? And then you suddenly find yourself living in half of a room, sharing a bathroom with strangers, constantly hearing the moaning and yelling common in nursing homes, and being surrounded by others who are past the possibility of independence. Imagine having to depend on nurses, aides, and orderlies for your daily activities: dressing, bathing, eating, or just getting around at times. Imagine dementia hindering your thought processes; imagine the overall confusion about where you are and why! How scary and unsettling that would be for most people! I know it would be for me!

A month and a half later, just before the Christmas holiday, we were told to expect her to be released within a week or two. Once again, the search was on to find Mom an assisted living facility since she could not function completely on her own. She especially needed assistance with dispensing her medications, and she no longer had meal preparation skills. Larry and I had also begun looking for a larger place to move, a home that had in-laws' quarters or one where they could easily be built on. With all the damage to area homes from the hurricanes, the search wasn't promising.

We found a facility that would take Mom into their full skilled unit first for a month and then relocate her to their assisted living apartments once it was deemed her wound had adequately healed, so we moved her immediately. Mom spent Christmas at the new facility. Larry and I volunteered our time and dressed the part of Santa and his elf, passing out presents to the residents at their Christmas party. This helped to draw Mom into their festivities to meet new people.

Finally Mom welcomed (with some resistance at first) the socializing and flurry of activities that were available. The facility offered services from different denominations on scheduled days each week, and she could participate in the services as she chose. Mom began regaining some of her strength and independence, but her dementia continued to worsen. Mom insisted that if she walked backwards, she'd get younger. She insisted that she was improving and soon would be able to drive again.

Although we knew the reality, we knew the path of least resistance when dealing with dementia, as with Alzheimer's patients, was agreement. If the dementia patient says, "I went shopping this morning and then had lunch with my friends," and you know that didn't happen, you should still say something like, "That's nice. Did you find any good sales?" You could tease the person about not spending too much rather than try to correct her and say, "No, you didn't." Correction brings on frustration and depression, and it's far easier to let the person make a safe place for herself. But also understand that if the person asks a direct question, she should be answered with the truth. She shouldn't be treated as if she is invisible.

Depending upon the extent of their dementia, such patients do hear and understand more than you may think. Individuals with dementia can have very lucid intervals when their cognition seems normal and intervals of living entirely in the alternative reality of their dementia. One of the many challenges of dealing with them is being able to change modes depending on the way the person is functioning minute to minute.

At first we thought relief was in sight. Mom was in a safe environment, happy, and her health was doing well for the most part. It was almost a year (and a blur at that) since this whole trajectory started; we learned quickly that it was not going to stop.

There's a horrible gray area once dementia begins taking hold. During this period, a person may exhibit behaviors that are the opposite of how she has acted most of her life. Mom had always been conservative, proper, strict, and frugal. Well, those traits went out the door. Let your imagination wander, and I'll bet you'll get a hint where this story is going.

Subscribe to the WIN Philosophy—<u>W</u>hat's <u>I</u>mportant <u>N</u>ow. When some life challenge seems overwhelming and you just don't know how you can continue, count your blessings, take a deep breath; and start your lists. The first list is the critical "right now" stuff; next is the lower priority; and then there's the "anything you just can't deal with right then and there but need to at some point" list. Cross through each item as you deal with it, and you will find that events aren't quite as overwhelming as they first seemed.

Chapter 4:
If Only Walking Backwards Somehow Worked

If—that small word has huge impact! In hindsight there are always things one could have done differently—but chances are you wouldn't have done them differently. Most likely your decisions were based on your morals, the information at hand, and what you believed to be the right approach at the time.

I've tried walking backwards and can't seem to get results. Oh, to be younger and have my health back. If only walking backwards could make me just a bit younger, I'd include it in my daily routine! I so needed the strength afforded by youth. I was an athlete all my life, and I found the events eroding my health hard to bear. I've always been one to persevere against opposition, though, so I persevered then.

As the sole surviving adult child in my family, I had to tackle this whole mess myself. For those of you with siblings, you might think siblings would make handling an aging parent's care easier. Each scenario, however, has its own disadvantages

Mom and Dad celebrated their fiftieth wedding anniversary several years before Dad passed away in 2001. They were a very devoted, loyal couple. Both were very conservative and found certain personality traits unacceptable. They had a strong religious base, and they were always there to help people in need. My brother and I grew up in a strict but loving family. We learned the difference between right and wrong. Trying to care for my mother, I ran up against one right/wrong issue that was very clear to me, but not to Mom in her diminished condition. This issue would prove very trying in the months ahead and is certainly a situation all too common with the elderly.

Parents and Predators

When I mentioned earlier that the pressures on me weren't going to ease up, that was somewhat of an understatement. Mom wasn't one to socialize much with other women. She and Dad were always together, and he was her focus. So when a man at the facility was attentive to her, she responded. For the sake of this story, I'll refer to him as LOOPIE (Living Off Other Peoples Income Everyday). She ate up his attention, but his character left much to be desired. Loopie had discovered that Mom had some money, and that was why he latched onto her. Loopie's previous lady friend was on her deathbed, and he needed to find a new source of income. Loopie wasn't unique to that facility either. You can probably find a Loopie in any of the facilities.

We made attempts to include him in various functions. We took him out to dinner with Mom and even had him over to our home on several occasions. After all, if Mom was finding some enjoyment, we were pleased. What a nightmare that connection turned out to be! And on top of it all, Loopie was rude and belligerent, but she would just laugh at his condescending comments, which further infuriated us. She accepted behavior from this man that she would never have tolerated before, and all because he was showing her attention—attention that was getting his way paid to dinner, to social events, shopping, and the like. Mom was buying his companionship and her independence, or so she thought. Employees at the facility witnessed her handing him money almost daily. They tried to talk with her about it, but that fell on deaf ears. Telling him he shouldn't take the money meant nothing to him. She simply started handing Loopie money covertly under the table instead of overtly over it. Beyond that, because she was in an assisted living facility and deemed competent, nothing could be done about him.

We found out that Loopie had brought home with him some pesky little visitors in the form of a highly contagious skin rash. Mom was treated by the facility's staff. We had to treat ourselves and sanitize everything. To our frustration, when Mom contracted it a second time, we learned that he had refused treatment. Yet he still was permitted to associate with the residents, including Mom. Mom insisted that he cared about her and that he was a good man. She said I was making things up.

When confronted on the moral issue of accepting money from Mom, Loopie acknowledged receiving the money but said that if she wanted to give it to him that was her choice. Once I had her voluntary guardianship, I tried to keep her on a reasonable budget, but he quickly decided that he didn't like my control over Mom's financial affairs and began working on her mentally and emotionally. During one lucid period, Mom had signed papers with an attorney, granting me a voluntary guardianship of her finances. Unfortunately she could revoke it at any time. Within months, Loopie convinced her to cancel it and took her to the attorney's office to do just that.

And I suppose you're wondering why I couldn't stop this. I tried— did I try! You see, her doctor at the facility at the time would give her a thirty-question mini-memory test to determine whether she was competent. If you aren't familiar with those, they ask a person's name, the date, the president, where they are, and similar questions. The tester doesn't spend more than about five minutes performing this test. Based on the percentage correct, they hand the person a piece of paper stating that he or she is competent. The test does not measure short-term memory or accurate perceptions of present reality.

Loopie knew the system and knew that he could take her to the bank and that nothing could be done. We talked with the Department of Children and Families, too. Their investigators looked into the situation. The outcome was the same. Mom had her doctor's certification indicating she was competent. The facility administration even filed complaints that also fell on deaf ears. I understand and appreciate that the legal system is in place to protect individuals and their rights, but I was having trouble understanding how it was protecting my mother's best interests.

That little piece of paper from the doctor stating she was competent was enough to tie the hands of her attorney, too. He requested a new statement from the doctor, but she still managed to answer accurately enough for the doctor to declare her competent. So with a stroke of the doctor's pen, she had complete control of her finances, a situation that gave her "friend" back his cash cow.

Mom also didn't have a driver's license since moving to Florida but insisted on keeping her car because she expected to be better and able to drive again. I tried on many occasions to explain rationally to Mom that she might not drive again. Her coordination was not up to par; there were other issues too.

"Mom," I'd ask her, "what if you couldn't brake fast enough and ended up hitting some children or taking the life of a mother? Is driving again worth that much to you?" Transportation was available should she desire to go somewhere. We could drive her, she could take a taxi, she could ride the bus that stopped in front of her facility, or she could use various senior driving services or private driving services. I'd mention these options while giving my rational explanation. However, rationality is not an accessible concept to a person with dementia.

Having made so many major changes to Mom's life recently, we reluctantly acceded to Mom keeping her car. She then let Loopie drive her car, unbeknownst to me at the time; and he did just that. He put the miles on it, too, and of course at her expense. Shortly after obtaining the guardianship, I discovered that her car insurance had lapsed. I was able to sell her car, as I could not justify the cost of maintaining the vehicle. Without a driver's license, she was unable to obtain insurance on her own, and I wasn't going to continue to have my name on the title of a car that her "friend" was going to drive. I didn't trust him, and within months my concerns would be justified.

Shortly after I sold her car, Loopie took Mom to a local dealership to purchase another new car. I had just been granted the guardianship and was in the process of changing accounts as required. The two of them withdrew enough funds from one bank to conclude the purchase. Immediately upon discovering this event, I presented myself and my official paperwork at the dealership, instructing them to take the vehicle back. They were very cooperative. My action did not sit well with Mom or her "friend." Once he was able to get her to cancel the guardianship, he took her back to the dealership, and she bought another brand-new car, putting his name on the title with rights of survivorship. This time I could not stop the transaction.

He also tried to convince Mom to sign the title over to him, because, as he put it, "It would be his anyway soon." Imagine him having the nerve to say that so brazenly, to me as well as to several others! Mom noticed that her car was gone one day. Unfortunately for him, she waited by the door and saw him return with another lady, which incited quite a scene at the facility. This discovery negated any thoughts she might have had of signing over the title to him.

Several months later, when we took possession of the car to sell it, we even discovered by accident that Mom had tried to drive her car on several occasions with him present. (Recall that she didn't have a driver's license). The car had a scrape on the bumper, so she must have run into something. Mom, sounding like a little kid, begged us not to tell her mom because she would get in trouble. (Her mother had passed away in the late 70s.)

Did I mention that Loopie drove a scooter? He initially had an older red scooter. Mom's preference was for blue—blue cars, blue flowers, blue clothes, and so on. She bought him a new blue scooter, which he kept for a short period of time. He wanted a red one again, though, and eventually managed to obtain enough money from Mom to trade the blue one in for a new red one.

When the car wasn't available for him to drive, Loopie convinced Mom to get on the back of the scooter, and off they would go. Did I mention that she was eighty-two at the time, barely able to walk with a walker, and always had hated motorcycles? Can you just picture the two of them on the scooter, sometimes with her walker mounted on the back? Oh, yeah—and we passed them one day as we were driving down the road. She was on the back of the scooter with a baseball cap on backwards! Don't get me wrong. I'm all for staying young at heart, active, and adventurous. But I had major concerns with her condition and the fact that she was riding with a seventy-eight-year-old man on a scooter in traffic on busy streets. I knew that drivers were often complacent about scooters and motorcycles. Mom's decision to ride with her friend on his scooter was far from logical, and I feared for her safety.

To make a long story short, despite ten thousand dollars in attorneys' fees and several investigations by the state through the Department of Children and Families, I could not put a stop to Mom's capricious spending, self-endangerment, and poor choice of male companions. Legally, as long as she was found competent by means of those thirty questions and that piece of paper, she could do whatever she wanted. She did not realize what was happening to her. She held fast to that piece of paper because that, in her mind, meant her independence. What a vicious circle. Since she had been found competent, I couldn't make her go to the doctor or specialist that she needed at the time. If she didn't want to go, there wasn't anything anyone could do or say to change that, yet it was obvious she wasn't being rational; she could not remember a conversation fifteen minutes later.

Mom's exploitative friend would work on her mentally and emotionally until she thought he was the only one she could trust. Others at the facility tried to talk with her too, but if he sensed her waffling, he would take her out and away from the facility for the day, running her ragged. Upon returning, she would barely have the strength to make it through dinner. He would purposely keep her away if he found out that the psychologist had an appointment scheduled with her. As her residence was an assisted living facility, the only requirement was that she sign herself out when leaving the facility and back in upon return. They could not restrict her from leaving or put any other restrictions on her as long as she was in control of herself. They were protecting her rights. She could refuse to see doctors if she wished. Her doctor wanted to treat her depression, but those efforts were rejected, too.

Periodically, Mom would have lucid moments and ask questions. When we would try to explain to her what she and her friend Loopie had been doing, her pat answer was either, "Why didn't someone tell me?" or "Why didn't you stop it?" She would then slip back into denial and do what she had done before.

To this day she gives the same response whenever her thoughts veer in those directions and questions arise. We generally try to deflect her questions, as it is pointless to resurrect those issues. We know that these discussions have a domino effect, and that she will become more anxious or depressed. Depression had plagued her since the death of my brother, whom she openly described as her favorite child since I so eagerly enjoyed the fishing and woodworking with Dad. My brother could do no wrong in her eyes, and the manner in which my brother died was more than she could accept.

Ten years later she still could not talk about him without tears. With the loss of her husband and now her diminishing health, Mom struggled painfully through the complicated web of depression. She continued to refuse treatment. Depression was one constant in this period of her life.

Money and difficulties with its management had also become constants in Mom's life. Three times over a two-year period, Mom changed banks and bank accounts, disrupting her Social Security direct deposits. Each time, the Social Security Administration was ready to cut off Mom's Medicare for lack of premium payments. Mom wasn't receiving her checks, and she couldn't understand why.

When Mom first moved to Florida, she requested that I become her representative payee with Social Security so that I could help deal with her finances and her Medicare paperwork. When disagreements arose, she asked me to remove myself from this role, which I did. However, when she supposedly appointed someone else, her money affairs were not managed. During a short lucid period, I discovered the declining situation of her finances. I gathered everything up and went to work sorting it all out, getting payments back on track and bills paid. It was shortly thereafter that Mom signed the voluntary guardianship papers designating me as guardian over her finances. Four months later, when she cancelled the guardianship, I again resigned as representative payee for Social Security. Both times, Social Security would send Mom letters, but she never did anything with them. Another three months or so passed, and her Social Security again was sitting in a dormant state. I received a call from the Social Security Office, asking me to step back into my role as representative payee. Their office tried to communicate with Mom, but without success. The representative explained that they had determined that Mom needed a representative payee, and it was in her best interest for me to resume that role. Reluctantly I agreed.

Mom changed banks after the guardianship was cancelled, and her pension checks from Dad's retirement with General Motors and other dividend checks, which had been directly deposited into her previous bank account, were also being sent back to the originators. (Her male friend had influenced her to move her money to the bank he utilized.)

Mom's phone was disconnected three or four times for nonpayment and incurred reconnection fees. There were a multitude of late fees, penalties, finance charges, and overdraft fees. One year she failed to file income taxes even though she swore she had done so. What an undertaking it was to reconstruct all her paperwork in order to file them a year later! Have I failed to mention that Mom and Dad never paid a late fee, finance charge, or overdraft fee in their fifty-two years of marriage? Their money was always accounted for to the penny!

At my attorney's recommendation, when she cancelled the guardianship, we finally had to say our prayers and just back away. Believe me, I've only touched the surface of all that occurred during that timeframe.

Just Another Wrinkle

I have one child of my own, and I never anticipated any disruption from him since he was busy with his own affairs. I could not have been more wrong about that, and the realization hit me harshly. The next two years were sheer hell that one no one should ever have to go through.

Suffering from dementia, my mother was easily swayed. My son, with the help of his new wife, thought they needed to become more actively involved in my mother's finances. Wrong. I got stuck in the middle of a power struggle: Mom wanting me out of her financial affairs and my son and his wife wanting into her financial affairs, which also included allegations through the Department of Children and Families. I felt like I was in the middle of Watergate and had to defend myself. I successfully defended myself but not without a price, both emotional and physical.

Several years have now passed, wounds have healed, apologies have been accepted, and my son has moved on in his life. My son is now thirty-one years old, and he has met a wonderful girl who will become his wife in the coming months. He also has accepted the shared responsibility of raising three adorable girls aged four, eight, and ten, which means I have three new granddaughters. My son has grown into a fine young man and found his way back to the person I always knew was inside.

When dealing with situations involving a loved one's financial activities, it is beneficial to keep good records and even sometimes document daily events in a journal. The information may prove invaluable should issues arise.

Chapter 5:
And Life Goes On

Did I mention that Larry was still hanging in there? Talk about a saint! He's been a real trooper and has been my strength when I thought I had none left. Friends and family members who had been following this scenario over the past couple of years have asked many times over why I didn't just walk away from Mom. I had made my Dad a promise before he died to take care of my mother. Dad understood only too well how difficult this task would be for me but also believed in the extent of my inner strength. I guess it's my upbringing—you just don't abandon your responsibilities, and that's all there is to it. And Larry didn't abandon me either.

About a year has passed since Mom "hit the wall," for lack of a better term. Her level of functioning had seriously declined further, and in a short period of time. At some point she suffered a mild heart attack and several small strokes, and it became obvious that her level of function had declined. The facility administration realized that she needed to move into the full skilled care side of the facility. Ironically, Mom had to acknowledge her difficulties and sign documentation admitting she recognized the same and that she needed full-time care. I don't know that she fully understood what was happening. Up until this point, that piece of paper stating that she was competent had kept her from getting the help she had so desperately needed.

Mom's so-called male companion quickly abandoned her when the money stopped flowing and the car disappeared. During several hospital stays, Mom would periodically ask where he was and didn't understand why he wouldn't visit her. We approached him on one occasion, asking him if he would assist her financially; she was his girlfriend, and her medical bills were accumulating. Loopie, true to form, indicated she wasn't his girlfriend. Showing signs of nervousness, he quickly walked away. After her last hospitalization before we moved her to a new facility, Loopie did make one additional effort, though. He tried to take Mom out of the nursing facility even though he had been told he was not permitted to do so. We had an alarm-signaling bracelet on Mom that would go off if she tried to exit without an aide silencing the alarm first. Luckily an aide stopped them. Mom could barely walk and wasn't sure where they were going. That wasn't too hard to figure out!

Knowing I needed to make some changes in her care, I found a new facility with extended congregate care much closer to our home. This facility had controlled access, a homelike atmosphere, and around-the-clock nursing care and aide support. Mom had her own studio apartment. She adjusted quickly to the change. Because her apartment was larger than her nursing home room, I was able to put more of her furniture in there, making it more homelike. Even after three years, though, her belongings from Ohio still occupied a huge storage unit.

As I recall, we managed twenty-four moves since 2004; I'm not counting the times the storage facility units had to be reorganized. Here's the list.

1) Ohio to the first rehabilitation facility

2) Remainder of items from Ohio taken to two air-conditioned storage units

3) Furniture taken to the first assisted living apartment

4-9) Room changes within the rehabilitation facility

10) Valuables from manufactured home to another storage unit in preparation for the hurricanes

11) Valuables back home after the hurricanes

12) Mom from the rehabilitation facility to assisted living apartment

13) Mom back to rehabilitation facility

14) Furniture from apartment back to storage

15) Two medium storage units to two larger units to accommodate the additional furniture

16) Mom to new nursing/rehabilitation facility

17) Mom to assisted living

18) More furniture from storage to her assisted living apartment

19) Our move to a new location after the hurricanes

20) Consolidation of storage unit contents into one large unit

21) Furniture to storage when moved back to nursing facility

22) Move to new assisted living apartment with full congregate care

23) Move to our current home

24) Clearing out storage units and moving contents to our new home

Phew! We should have started our own moving business!

If I may digress a moment, remember our original plan when we brought Mom to Florida: we would get a bigger place, preferably a house with an in-law suite or one that we could modify to afford her some privacy and independence. Well, with all the hurricane damage and then Mom settling in and liking her assisted living placement, primarily because of one particular male person, as we found out later, those arrangements never occurred. The large truckload of furnishings from Ohio remained in several storage units, racking up quite hefty fees and late charges over several years. Because she was negligent in her payments, the storage facility had locked out her unit and was preparing to initiate an auction. We stepped in and paid the three months' storage fees and penalties to prevent that action.

As if we weren't having enough fun, Larry had his own medical battles; a large 8mm kidney stone embedded in the wall of the kidney will definitely cause excruciating pain. He also had a severe bout with poison ivy, reacting negatively to the treatment and then also discovering the poison ivy spores had affected his lungs. Add to that a heart catheterization done as a precaution after he somehow failed a stress test when he couldn't breathe because of the poison ivy spores in his lungs. Poor guy—he was truly miserable.

In the latter part of 2007, after moving Mom to the new facility, we felt that our affairs were going in the right direction again. We had to deal with several serious health issues upon Mom leaving the previous facility, but the new staff was very compassionate and understanding. Mom had been negligent in obtaining the proper medical attention, so I immediately made arrangements with a dermatologist I knew. Mom had to be quarantined for almost three weeks due to a condition she contracted at the previous facility. Mom eventually pulled through, but not without increased depression and confusion. She was also diagnosed with a somewhat rare skin disorder. Luckily her skin disorder is not contagious, and we are able to manage its periodic flare-ups.

We quickly developed relationships with the staff and administration at her new facility, and those relationships really helped. Tackling one issue at a time, I eventually managed to have Mom seen by a cardiologist, a neurologist, a new general practitioner, a podiatrist, a dentist, and an optometrist.

She kept having falls. Her trips to the emergency room became more frequent, almost weekly for several months. Her blood pressure wasn't stable and would spike. Protocol required a trip to the ER when this occurred.

The scenario gets better yet. As many nursing homes did after the first of the year, the new facility reduced their staff due to the economy. Mom's blood pressure would usually rise late in the evening, and the aide would call the nurse on call. The nurse would call the doctor, and the doctor would instruct them to send Mom to the ER. At first they called an ambulance to transport her, but after several trips, I stepped in and insisted they call us first. We lived five minutes away and could get there faster than the ambulance, then transport her the two blocks to the hospital. When she went by ambulance, the ambulance company would submit the bill to Medicare with a note that the transport wasn't medically necessary. Such trips were not covered by Medicare or her supplemental insurance, so she would get billed nearly five hundred dollars for a two-block ride. The frequency of the trips increased. Generally we would get the call after 11:00 PM, which meant sitting in the ER four or five hours and then having to be bright-eyed and bushy-tailed for work in the morning.

As we started researching the situation more, we found that Mom would have pain in her arms and legs because she would lie across her bed in an awkward position, causing her limbs to become numb. On any given day, if asked if she had pain, her answer was always "Yes." After all, she had had shoulder surgeries and two knee replacements, and there were all those falls. When the aide would ask where she had pain, Mom would tell them that she had pain in her arm and that her fingers were numb.

Pain causes the blood pressure to rise, and heart problems are the first possibility that comes to mind. I understood the liability issues and tried to show patience. With so many trips to the ER, the doctors soon had a baseline and found that if they gave her a Tylenol when she first arrived, the pain would subside, and her blood pressure would return to normal within a half hour. It was during this period that I found a new cardiologist for her, too. I also found out that her new doctors avoided prescribing pain pills for patients suffering from dementia, as the medication generally magnifies confusion and agitation.

I'm happy to say that we are very pleased with her new doctors. Her new cardiologist has modified her medications, and Mom's blood pressure has remained stable and well within range for the most part. It tends to rise only when there is another underlying problem.

Having a family plan that addresses an elder's health care needs will minimize unnecessary expenses and chaos that may be associated with the uncertainties of lifestyle adjustments.

Chapter 6:
A New Dawn

We were reaching our saturation point where exhaustion was concerned, like a flooded lowland that couldn't possibly be any wetter. We were trying to manage our own health issues, and our health issues and Mom's were both subject to the domino effect: when something bad happened, another bad development followed in short order. Mom ended up hospitalized for a week twice within the first two months of 2008 and had numerous other runs to the ER within that period. As we were finishing dinner one night, our conversation focused on what could be done to change this spiraling situation. We stumbled on a possibility that we thought just might work, and the next day, we put our plan into action.

Within two weeks, we found a new house, made an offer, and were able to secure occupancy within thirty days. Remember my style of confronting challenges? Once taking occupancy, we had thirty days more to ready the house—we were moving Mom in with us.

Who's got the two-by-four? I'm standing steady as I can and bracing for the impact! You see, there's one other small detail I previously mentioned although I skirted it somewhat. It is true that we grew up in a strict and loving environment, but Mom also favored my brother all my life. She and I have had a rocky relationship as long as I can remember, with admitted jealousy over my relationship with my dad. It seemed I could never do anything right in her eyes. Once I even got berated for not parking the car with the tires facing straight ahead; I had left them turned. Yet, through the years, I was always the one called when there were problems and emergencies.

I grew up a tomboy. I loved sports and fishing and always latched onto Dad as his helper around the house. Larry and I have a little joke between us. He discovered early in our relationship that I knew how to drill pilot holes when he was trying to shortcut a project. Not only did I know about pilot holes, but I baited hooks, wired electrical outlets, had decent woodworking skills, and could disassemble and reassemble mechanical things. These interests led me to hang out with my dad. Poor Larry never had a chance to dazzle me with his projects and tools.

I've always been taught to take the high road in situations, and Larry is a strong supporter of that philosophy as well. Mom is family, and I was always taught that family takes care of one another. I knew it was wrong for me to let her just exist in her present situation when I had the ability to make some changes and do what I knew was right. Trust me, I had to dig deep after the many somewhat volatile years between myself and my mother, including the past several years' events, to take this one on. I had to accept that we would be living under the same roof—not separate living spaces either, where I could leave and go back to the sanctuary of my own place. My decision was truly a life-changing event for me—and yet also another emotional upheaval. I needed to find forgiveness within myself and move on. I had to let go of resentment I harbored and dig deep, and I did. This was going to be yet another major challenge largely because of Mom's failing health.

I've mentioned what a saint Larry is. I still don't know what I would do without him! We have come to the conclusion that our dads, Dick and Ed, were sitting at the edge of a lake up in Heaven and fishing. As fishermen do, they struck up a conversation, and they decided that Larry and I would be good for each other—we both would need someone just as supportive to face our approaching challenges. We met, and the rest is history.

What is Mom's status at this time? Mom uses a wheelchair and can only move it by shuffling her feet. She cannot stand up by herself; she cannot walk on her own, and she suffers from incontinence, common at this stage. She has limited mobility in her arms and requires assistance with eating and other activities throughout the day, more on some days than on others. Mom's left hand does not operate very well, but she can still eat with her right hand.

Initially I scheduled a home healthcare agency to come and assess her for therapy. Therapy commenced the first week Mom moved into our home and continued for several weeks thereafter. Mom has had two hospital stays since moving in with us. A home health care agency has also followed her progress for several weeks after she was discharged. Each time she has received several weeks of physical therapy.

Larry volunteered to deal with Mom during the day while I was working. At first Mom seemed embarrassed, but Larry quickly reminded her that "this wasn't his first rodeo." Larry had cared for his mother and grandmother together at one point in his life. He handled my mother with dignity and respect, and she quickly grew to accept his care.

I arranged for a couple of women to assist us several hours in the afternoon so that Larry and I could get away for a few hours to go shopping, to dinner, or elsewhere when my work day ended. We've been lucky when it came to finding caregivers. We talked with one of the aides from her former residential facility, an aide whom Mom really liked. She was good with Mom and luckily welcomed some additional time with Mom.

We feel very blessed to have the help we have. They are good with Mom and assist in performing her daily exercises prescribed by the therapists. We are very comfortable leaving each day, knowing they are trustworthy and very attentive to her needs. They are very good at keeping Mom and her sitting area clean; they wash the dishes they use; they empty the garbage daily. They do some moderate cleaning, including her bathroom as needed, bathe her according to the schedule, and take her for walks around the neighborhood.

We refer to Mom's bath days as her "spa days." She feels pampered, and it helps to lift her spirit. Her spa days also help with circulation and other body functions, ultimately easing stress on us too. Mom has always preferred to be the center of attention; when she is not getting attention, she tends to display some undesirable personality traits. Mom remains comfortable with the level of attention provided by the caregivers. This care also reduces her need for our constant attention.

Larry continues to be extremely helpful during the day with her.

He gets her up and ready in the morning, generally singing to her and joking. Mom sometimes sings along with him. She says she feels like a drunken sailor as he helps her walk from her bed to the bathroom, so they sing an old Irish song about a drunken sailor every morning. She's even made her own verse.

I make her breakfast in the mornings and then go off to my part of the house to work in my office. She likes her naps, and she loves sitting outside when the weather permits. Larry takes her out in the car if he has errands to run—"running the roads," as they call it. We take her out to breakfast on weekends, and I generally take her to visit my son once a week. Going out, she gets a change of scenery and some additional activity, which is so necessary for the body at any age.

Mom loves watching the reality dance shows and always wants us to "put on the dance channel." Larry generally puts music on for her to listen to while eating breakfast (big band or easy listening). Just the other morning, as I walked past her sitting area, I stopped to watch them. While transferring Mom from her wheelchair to the couch, Larry held her up in a dance position while she shuffled her feet to the music. Just picture a 6'6" man dancing with a 4'10" frail older lady—but their dance made her morning. Later I could hear her singing to one of the songs; I'm sure it brought back memories. This too needs to be monitored, though, as too much reflection back to past memories may cause depression, but this tendency is generally easy enough to deflect with other activity.

The food programs are always a good fallback and pique her interest. We have learned to refrain from having news on her TV, however. She will focus on one subject that evokes memories, and this focus may bring on a panic attack. She has lost the concepts of relative locations and time, and she fears that everything she hears on TV is happening right outside. On the bright side, Mom has begun to enjoy watching football again. She has been a sports enthusiast (and a star basketball player in high school) all her life. Go Buckeyes!

And the large storage unit that held her belongings from Ohio? You guessed it! I've been able to eliminate some of its contents, but most of her stuff is in her rooms, in our garage (where there is no room for cars), or in the attic storage to be dealt with sometime in the future.

At least once a week, Mom will ask where Dad, her mother, and my brother are, not remembering that they passed away. She expects me to tell her particulars, and it upsets her that she doesn't remember their passing. This conversation was very hard for me the first few times. Since then, I've learned to give a condensed version and then to change the subject completely and get her mind on something else.

For now, life is moving forward. Quite frankly, once we got our basic daily routine down, having Mom onsite and being able to control her care, maintain her personal hygiene, and minimize her exposure to other health hazards, not to mention my learning to forgive her, all have played a significant role in reducing the stress in our lives. Managing her care is not as disruptive of our daily routines as I initially imagined it might have been.

> **Although one may never forget, it is important for one's own well-being to forgive.**

Part Two:

The Action Plan

Chapter 7:
Where to Begin

I have made the last page of my book available for you to jot down your own personal notes as you continue through the remaining pages. As thoughts come to you while reading, make notes to jog your mind later.

First and foremost, families need to know what they are going to do if a vulnerable family member becomes incapable of self-care. No one wants to talk about this situation, but it is less painful and stressful if a plan for dealing with it is already in place, and not just for the sake of an elderly parent. For such a situation, we all need a plan. A plan starts with legal documentation.

Important documents to execute include the following:

- a simple will (at the minimum)
- durable power of attorney (POA)
- healthcare surrogate and durable power of attorney for healthcare
- living will

An attorney can easily draw up the necessary documents, though software is also available if you would like to do so yourself. Many states' departments of motor vehicles also have the forms available and can provide notary services too. Whichever path you utilize, having these documents available will benefit you tenfold should there be an event that requires these documents. I keep copies of the documents on me in the event of a situation that would necessitate their use. Before relocating Mom to Florida, I always kept these documents readily available, even when I traveled. Having them available has saved time and frustration on more than one occasion.

Now suppose that you are dealing with an aging parent who recognizes his or her need for help with finances and that there is concern over access to that parent's funds. In this situation, in states that recognize voluntary guardianships, an attorney may execute a voluntary guardianship. It is important to understand, however, the complications and responsibilities that come with the guardianship. There are court proceedings to grant the guardianship even though it is voluntary and for finances only and not a full guardianship over the person. There are initial financial statements required, including an initial inventory of assets; reconciliation of expenditures and funds; yearly reports to the courts; training one must take within a prescribed period of time of being named the guardian; a bond that must be posted; and statutes that one must adhere to in handling the finances. Then all financial accounts are renamed to reflect the guardianship. The courts can grant the guardianship to a family member, to an attorney, or anyone else who demonstrates the ability to handle the finances appropriately. This can become a costly avenue. On the upside, if there are concerns about someone accessing funds inappropriately, this avenue will offer an additional level of protection.

If you are just taking care of your parent and there are no other issues of concern, the voluntary guardianship can be cumbersome and costly when it comes to managing their affairs. If the proper documents have been executed and some preplanning has been accomplished, the transfer of responsibility should have minimal impact. Keep good records of expenses and always consult the appropriate professionals to help guide you through situations. Most information can be obtained just by asking questions; in other cases, it may be necessary to pay for professional services.

If you are the primary caregiver for a parent, having your name added jointly to banking accounts will ease the burden as the transition of financial responsibilities occurs. This change makes it easier to pay bills, close accounts if you have to relocate your parents, or secure funds for their needs if they become incapacitated. My mother added me to her accounts after my dad passed away. I never utilized my ability to access the accounts until my mom's accident, and the need arose for me to step in. I know there are many times when a parent won't do this for one reason or another. If the relationship between the parent and adult child is one of trust and the child is assuming the parent's financial affairs for ethical reasons, it is the best way to go.

If your parents have stocks or other holdings, I would advise you to address these early on, planning how they will be transferred and to whom. It is always advisable to consult with a family planning attorney, an accountant, or a representative of the holding company or brokerage firm to understand all your options and their implications before making changes.

Although it appears Mom did many of the right things to organize her finances, stubbornness and paranoia made her refuse to hire an expert to assist with her estate planning. Due to her secrecy and resistance to the idea of anyone meddling in her finances, some decisions she made have now come to hurt her financially. Add the fact that as a spouse supported by my father's pension, effective the first of 2009, along with millions of other retirees and/or affected spouses of General Motors retirees, she lost her health insurance. That loss meant that I had to seek out new supplemental coverage to augment her Medicare. That endeavor can be an extremely confusing and time-consuming task.

The more involved you become, the more you will understand that the single most important and powerful piece of paperwork needed is the durable power of attorney (POA). Always keep your certified, original copy in a safe place and several copies on hand. I also found it a good idea to have several certified copies of the original. There are situations where a recipient will want more than just a regular photocopy.

The POA can also be recorded in the courts, which substantiates it further. This step will generally be required if you are involved in a real estate transaction. The title company will accomplish this for you if it is not already recorded. Most state laws require that a durable POA be recognized even though you may come across some situations in which it is challenged and have to insist on its acceptance. There are situations, though, in which some companies or agencies will require their own POA form to be executed and will not accept what you have. I suppose this could be contended. However, proper planning early on will identify requirements. Once executed as required, the POA will remain on file unless it is withdrawn by the person initiating the authority.

Second to the durable POA is the durable POA for healthcare. This is also a must, especially if dealing with doctors and hospitals. Without this document, it will be difficult to accomplish certain actions that may be required on your parent's behalf due to the Privacy Act or to solidify certain requests for records, treatment, signature authority for medical procedures, consultation with the medical providers, and others.

You must also make a thorough exploration of Social Security and Medicare. Your parent can request that you become her representative payee. Once you are the representative payee, the checks will come to you for "your parent's name" via direct deposit into an account at the bank. A statute requires that they be deposited into an account that the person does not have the ability to access. The funds are to be utilized towards the person's monthly expenses. Once a year, the representative payee will receive a simple form to complete, attesting to those expenditures. Being representative payee will also open the doors for dealing with their Medicare information. Visit your local Social Security office for more information. Information is also available at Social Security Online, www.ssa.gov.

Just by accomplishing these few simple tasks, events that are inevitable will become more manageable than not, even at a time of chaos. Again, if unsure, it is always wise to consult with the professionals: an attorney, an accountant, a banker, the holding company of the stocks. Do your research and collect your information first. Then proceed according to your particular needs and situation.

While your parent(s) still have their capacities, try to understand their files. Learn where they keep documents such as wills, life insurance policies, and the like. My mother was a bookkeeper for years before I was born, but after Dad passed away, she found it difficult to keep up with technology. She still kept her records in longhand, with handwritten notes all over her documents. I took the time to create an electronic spreadsheet with pertinent information regarding her accounts, their locations, specific notes, and the like, and placed it in her files. I kept a copy for quick reference when needed. Although at the time I developed a huge headache, fearing what was down the road, doing this helped me understand what I needed to know. At the same time, she was able to continue maintaining her files in the way that made her comfortable. If you do your detective work, the baselines you establish regarding your parent's affairs and medical situations will ultimately be very important down the road.

Managed Facilities vs. In-home Care

Making a decision about an elder's move to a safer environment is a major event. It doesn't happen easily, as commitment to and acceptance of these inevitable decisions are difficult for most people. There will be controversy as well as apprehension. Being persistent and reinforcing that change is in the parent's best interest and for the sake of safety is sometimes all that can be done. Far too often, the need for the move develops suddenly. Emphasize the idea of having more enjoyable time with friends and less worry about upkeep. Try to develop a list of pros and cons and show the parent examples of the new experiences possible in a safer place. Eventually, and hopefully without experiencing a life-threatening emergency as in my mother's case, your parent will yield to your pleas.

When trying to make a decision which will best suit your situation, make sure to do your homework thoroughly. Relocating a parent to a nursing facility or even in an assisted living facility may initially seem to be the most logical and stress-free path for the involved family members. There are other issues to consider that I originally did not understand. I would suggest making several inquires when considering a facility. Ask how they screen their workers. Find out to what extent they check references of potential employees. Ask how they verify past employment and measure an applicant's present skills and if they screen for criminal activity. Ask if they drug-test their candidates or if they periodically drug-test employees. These are all very relevant issues when considering placement at a facility.

When your parent (or other loved one) enters a facility, you basically lose control. Once under the control of the facility, the person falls under the guidelines of the state statutes. Although a person's rights as an individual are protected, you need to ask yourself if placing that person in a situation that maintains his or her complete independence and restricts your assistance is in the person's best interest at this point. Once your parent has entered a facility (assisted living, skilled nursing or similar type facilities), that's exactly what happens. If a person's capacities are diminishing and he or she can't completely take care of personal needs and you are aware that this person is unable to make rational decisions, why would you then put the person into a situation where you lose your ability to provide the necessary guidance to support her or his well-being? By putting your parent in a facility, you lose that control; you also ultimately inherit any problems that occur and are expected to clean them up.

Don't assume that your parent is properly protected in a facility. If not in control before entering the facility, why would your parent become the best judge of right and wrong once there? For example, many states have a law regarding sex in residential and nursing facilities. Although we want our parents to be happy and enjoy their remaining time on this earth, if they have entered these facilities because they are not able to take proper care of themselves, does it make sense to assume that they still understand right and wrong or the medical implications of various activities—or even care, for that matter? Did you know that recent reports indicate that sexually transmitted diseases (STDs) are on the rise, and that there is actually an increase found in nursing facilities? In some states, if you go into a room at a facility and two consenting elderly adults are having sex, you must turn around and leave until they are done. Let's see. They can't take care of themselves and they have trouble accomplishing daily activities … but okay, what's a little sex, right? They might be having protected sex, but it's not because they're using a condom!

Just prior to George Bush leaving office, a new law, without congressional debate or public knowledge, was signed into effect. This new law makes it almost impossible for the public to have access to inspection reports on nursing facilities, as reported by *The Washington Post* on February 24, 2009. This law makes it more difficult for families to be aware of irresponsible practices. I would suggest consulting with an attorney who specializes in this area regarding any concerns you might have. Also, there are many websites that can provide additional guidance on such regulations and various legal issues related to nursing facilities. You can also refer to the 1987 Nursing Home Reform Act for additional information.

Should a parent reside in a facility, they may opt to utilize the physician associated with that facility. Sadly, from my experience, the physicians associated with facilities are not as ambitious as other doctors one may independently utilize. True, it is convenient to use the associated physician if your parent resides in a facility, but it may turn out to not be in your parent's best interest. Each needs to be judged independently, so be assertive; participate in the parent's care and question situations as you feel necessary. You almost have to become a detective to help yourself manage a parent's affairs. Remember, as your parent ages and has increasing difficulty thinking and remembering, he or she may appreciate some help from you in understanding medical needs.

Investigate the state laws governing any facility you are considering, including the laws on residents' rights.

Chapter 8:
Becoming the Primary Caregiver

Okay, you've taken the plunge. What now? It's time to get organized. Moving your parent into your home, developing a routine, and delegating chores will enable life to continue with minimal impact. There are a multitude of websites and publications that can provide information to assist you with your adventure. There are also local home health care agencies that provide medical assistance once your parent becomes established with them. They require minimal effort to get started, and the majority of the cost is covered by Medicare and insurance. They will come to your house and file all the paperwork. You can also find a wealth of information and support through the Eldercare Locator, a free national service of the Administration on Aging at www.eldercare.gov. The National Council on Aging at www.ncoa.org and AARP at www.aarp.org are also good organizations from which to obtain information. Most all major areas have local councils on aging too. If your parent has been hospitalized, the hospital's social worker can also recommend local support in your area.

As elders' health changes, often so does their ability to balance. It's hard to accept the transition from walking independently to utilizing a cane or a walker, but safety is of the utmost importance. If your parent doesn't already have a walker and needs one, check your local

Goodwill, Salvation Army, thrift stores, or classified advertisements for used ones first. There are tons of them out there. If one is bought secondhand, make sure it is safe to use and in good condition. One can also be obtained through Medicare/Medicaid, but obtaining one through those agencies may trigger further restrictions on the ability to obtain a wheelchair down the road if one is needed. Local medical supply companies can guide you through this process.

From a membership-required discount store, we obtained a walker with wheels and a seat. They can also be purchased in many local drug stores. Mom used it for a couple of years. That was the best investment and enabled her to feel more independent. She always had a place to sit if she tired from walking, and she had a basket under the seat to carry things. These walkers easily fold for loading in a vehicle, but beware—they come with pockets too! As people age, some start hording things, and those pockets become hazardous when loaded with sugar, opened creamers, jelly, note paper, pens and pencils, Kleenex, candy (including melted chocolate), and pamphlets! These items that they collect can make for a gooey mix! And while on that note, keep an eye out for "goodies" hidden in drawers—rotten bananas, moldy food, and clothing don't mix!

If your parent needs a wheelchair, there are several issues to consider. For a person who is still very active and alert, a power chair is a great way to go. There are local stores that advertise assistance in obtaining power chairs, and it is possible that up to 100% of the cost may be covered by Medicare or Medicaid. Always check. Generally a folding travel wheelchair will also be provided as part of the package. Should your parent's physical condition decline to a point where they can no longer use the power chair, the only way to obtain a regular wheelchair covered by Medicare or Medicaid is to return the power chair. There are time restrictions that may come into play if the transition is only within a couple of years. Again, ask questions.

Some people may opt to purchase a wheelchair apart from Medicare or their insurance. Keep the receipts because medical supplies may be tax-deductible at the end of the year. Tax deductions may also be taken for any modifications done to your home to accommodate your parent. Ask a tax consultant to provide guidance on permissible deductions and proper documentation for them.

Your parent may also benefit by having a hospital bed at home. This equipment can be also be obtained through a medical supplier and covered by Medicare or Medicaid. As incontinence sets in, the vinyl mattress is a lifesaver and can be easily cleaned. Changing the bed linens daily, you will come to appreciate this type of bed. Also, your parent will begin to need a lower bed to sit on with ease. At this juncture, a person does not need anything larger that a twin-size bed. With a twin bed, it is much easier to assist them with bedtime activities or if their health fails, restricting their daily activity.

I also obtained from the medical supplier an adjustable-height bed tray on wheels (much like those used in the hospital) which sits nicely next to Mom's bed at night and in front of her on the couch if she wants during the day.

When looking through those catalogues that always seem to clutter our mailbox, I noticed a bed pad with extended sides for tucking under the mattress. I purchased two of them (they are quite inexpensive) so that I had an alternate. They have a plastic underside that helps to minimize bed linen changes. I also purchased a couple of extra smaller pads to use on the chair or couch where Mom sits. Be sure that pads have a plastic back, or they may still leak through if there is an accident. Putting a large garbage bag around the cushion first and then putting the chair pad under a decorative sheet will save a lot of extra cleanup, not to mention preserving the condition of your furniture. We also keep a supply of disposable bed pads on hand. You may notice cycles when the added protection is necessary.

When incontinence is present, the transition to disposable adult pull-ups is extremely beneficial. We buy them in bulk from the membership-required discount store. You can also arrange for them to be delivered to your home from a mail-order supply house.

Diving in Head First

Unless other family members are willing to take a turn and provide some routine break time, definitely consider securing some additional help, if for no other reason than to get a sanity check. We all think we are superhuman, but even Superman and Wonder Woman need a break now and then! Timeouts aren't just for disciplinary problems either.

When being the primary caregiver, a timeout may mean attending functions at an affiliated church or support groups in your local area related to your parent's situation, such as Alzheimer's support groups, cancer support groups, and various support functions. It's always good to find out that you're not alone.

Local area organizations also provide day care options in most communities. These are usually on scheduled days and hours. Day care also can provide some down time should you need to run errands. Additionally, many times local nursing facilities offer respite care; your parent could stay overnight or for several days if you need to be out of town. Respite care is another alternative to consider.

We have assistance several days a week. Those few hours each day afford us time to get away and go shopping, go to dinner, see a movie, or go to the gym. At times we struggle to find something that will keep us away from the house, but by the same token, it has motivated us to find new interests to share. Other times we may come home early and work on projects around the house. It's just nice having those few hours every day to come and go and not have to worry about one person staying behind or loading Mom up in the car with her wheelchair, since we can't leave her alone. I haven't yet decided who is more taxing at times—a three-year-old or an eighty-five-year-old!

Visiting nursing agencies exist in every community and provide assistance at comparable rates. When utilizing an agency, generally there is less flexibility in hourly support; possibly a requirement for more hours than needed; and a higher rate of pay than if you take a little extra time to explore hiring an independent caregiver. Explore the advertisements in the classified section of your local newspaper. Caregivers will advertise their services soon after losing someone they have cared for or to pick up additional hours to supplement their income. Check their references. Acquaintances in the health field can also be a good source in finding caregivers. Nursing students may be interested in working a few hours and as an added bonus may also get some study time in, depending upon the level of care needed.

By talking to a few caregivers, one can find out the going hourly rate. Licensed caregivers such as certified nursing assistants (CNAs) and registered nurses may require a higher rate of pay. There are generally quite a few unlicensed caregivers and retired nurses with many years of service who are very capable. Again, agencies will always cost more than caregivers who are not registered with an agency, but you may feel more comfortable utilizing the agency's services. Agencies' standards may be so variable that I would suggest asking how they screen their workers, what reference checks they perform, and how they verify past employment. You may also want to find out how they measure the present skills of their employees and if they screen for criminal activity and drug-test candidates. If you choose to not utilize an agency, do your homework and check references of prospective candidates. There are no guarantees with either. Making inquiries will help you to decide which way best serves your needs.

The Extra Little Things

To help Mom remember which caregiver is coming each day, I made simple cards with each of their photos and names. I found a plastic picture holder that stands on the table. I rotate their ID cards in the holder. Mom has found this to be very helpful and takes comfort in being able to refer to the cards, especially when she forgets who they are or their names.

Ask your parent's family doctor about getting set up with a home healthcare service in your area. The process is very easy, and once you are registered with a particular healthcare service, their nursing assistance is available via the telephone 24/7. Through the doctor's recommendation, the home health care services will make arrangements to come to your home, assess your parent's condition, and provide recommendations on the services they can provide to assist with your parent's care.

It's advisable to ask the doctor to request therapy. Home health care agencies will provide physical and occupational therapy, depending upon your parent's needs. The therapists will also gladly recommend ways to assist your parent through normal daily activities. Additionally, it can be difficult to take your parent to a lab for blood work and other tests, and the home healthcare agency can be very helpful, sending a nurse to your home to draw blood if necessary and deliver it to the lab for evaluation. Most of this service is covered by Medicare/Medicaid and also by your parent's supplemental insurance if they have it. Generally small co-payments will be billed. We have found the home healthcare agency nurses to be extremely helpful, kind, and compassionate. They have a wide range of services and can provide helpful ways to support daily tasks.

Items of Necessity

Toiletries Set aside a closet or cupboard, preferably near the bathroom your parent will be using or in their bedroom, to store toiletries and basic medical supplies. Include items such as lotions, powders, antibiotic cream, cotton balls, and bandages. These should be items specific to your parent's needs so that the caretaker has quick and easy access to the items and does not have to search through the house for them.

Plastic gloves Always have a box of plastic surgical gloves on hand. These can be obtained from the drug store or your local discount department store. If you have additional help, they too will want to utilize the gloves and will be grateful because you have them available. I have also found it very beneficial to carry a small plastic lunch bag in my purse with a pair in case of necessity when I have Mom away from the house. By such simple planning and care to maintain sanitary conditions, the unpleasant situations are manageable.

Hand sanitizer Keep a bottle of hand sanitizer available to help prevent cross-contamination. I actually went one step further and found a small, inexpensive wall-mounted dispenser for hand sanitizer. We mounted this dispenser just outside Mom's bathroom, low enough that Mom can reach it. She finds it fascinating to use the foamy sanitizer sometimes, and we and our caregivers utilize it too.

Blood pressure unit Consider purchasing a blood pressure unit from your drug store. They are relatively inexpensive and very easy to use, automatically displaying blood pressure and pulse readings. They come in handy, especially if dealing with any high blood pressure issues, sickness, or requests from the doctor to monitor blood pressure for a few days when changing medications.

Tableware When our grandson was younger, we had purchased a plastic cup with a screw-on lid and a "straw" as part of the handle. These come in a multiple of colors and can be found in the plastic tableware section of your local discount department store. I purchased additional ones for Mom, as they are extremely easy for her to use, and having a lid eliminates spills. She drinks through the top of the handle like a straw.

Mom also loves the colorful plastic divided plates made for children. She eats very small portions, and the small divided sections help her to pick up her food. I also obtained several rectangular break-proof plates. These work well too; she doesn't have to reach as far to get to her food.

Detergent and bleach for soiled laundry This should be common sense but is worth mentioning. When dealing with soiled laundry from your parent, establish a rule to launder those items separately in hot water. My washer has a sanitizing setting that has been very useful. I use white sheets on Mom's bed so they can be bleached and generally have a flowered pillow case to accent her blue quilt. The thin white cotton blankets, much like those used in the hospital, are great to use too and wash up easily. I always use either regular bleach or color-safe bleach as appropriate when doing her laundry.

Medical information and daily status We quickly found how important it was to simplify our new responsibilities by organizing information and tasks. Whether during a stressful situation or just a routine visit to a doctor, the medical information necessary can be mind-boggling even for someone without the added responsibilities. The recommendations and forms I provide herein will ultimately lessen your stress levels, reduce frustrations, and ease anxiety at moments when chaos erupts.

I recommend the purchase of a 9" x 12" three-ring binder with pockets on the inside front and back covers to organize the following forms, along with a package of tabbed section dividers. I also suggest purchasing an 8 ½" x 11" business card holder sheet. They come pre-punched for three-ring binders and are a convenient way to maintain all pertinent business cards for the various doctors and other contacts. The binder makes it easy to keep daily logs and other information readily available in one place.

Place a manila envelope in the front pocket of the folder with "FOR EMERGENCIES" written boldly across the front. Anyone in the household should be made aware of the envelope. In the event of an emergency, it can be handed to the ambulance team or to the nurse at the hospital.

In the envelope, include:

- Copy of the driver's license or state identification card*
- Copy of the insurance card(s)—front and back*
- Copy of the Medicare card (and Medicaid if applicable)*
- Copy of the Do Not Resuscitate (DNR) form if one has been executed. Original should be taped to the refrigerator. (This document must be executed and signed by the doctor and the person or his or her legal representative.)
- Copy of the durable POA for healthcare
- Copy of the living will if one has been executed
- Current copy of the information and diagnosis form (below)

*It's always a good idea to carry either the original cards or a copy either on you or in your vehicle, should they be needed.

Doctor's information form Complete the list of the prescribed medications. Keep this form current as medications change. This form will be invaluable when taking your parent to the doctor or to the hospital. When going on a planned trip to the doctor's office, include at the bottom any additional pertinent information, such as blood pressure and pulse readings from the last few days or so, body temperature over the past several hours/days, or any symptoms that may be the reason for the visit.

Medical information form Compile all medical history and personal information. When asked to fill out or provide the medical history, I just hand this form to the nurse or attach it to the paperwork when going to the hospital or to a doctor for the first time. It is also very helpful to hand off to a visiting home healthcare provider.

Daily Log Sheet I have learned from experience that this is very valuable to have. Doctors, emergency room nurses, caregivers, or home healthcare providers will appreciate having this information readily available when dealing with the elderly. This document also minimizes errors when dispersing prescribed medications and affords you the ability to watch intakes and to know where dosages may need adjustment. At any time something additional is added, such as an antacid, those extra medications should also be written in and managed in the same fashion on that day. Food and liquid amounts can be estimated unless there are very strict diet restrictions provided by your parent's physician. I have also found it invaluable to refer back to various days/patterns when questions are posed by her physician when diagnosing a problem. One time it was even helpful when he needed to refer to situations several months back. After a few days utilizing the sheet, it will become part of the routine.

If you have caregivers who assist with your parent's care, documentation also provides accountability for actions taken or tasks accomplished during their shift. Healthcare professionals are used to logging this type of information, so it will be easy for them. Insist that your caregiver(s) utilize the form.

When using a daily log sheet, keep a highlighter handy and highlight the times identified when each medication is given or simply cross through the time. I prefer the highlighter because it is easy to glance at the sheet and notice if something is due or has not been administered and vice verse. Always check with others attending if it appears something has been missed before administering a medication. It may be that they just forgot to mark off the time. This record will provide you or anyone else a good check and balance. Trust me, you will find that this form is one of your best friends.

Should you have to transport your parent to the emergency room, take the daily log sheet for the nurse to photocopy. If it is current, this log will let the medical personnel know about your parent's food and medication intake, information that can be very important for the doctor.

General information sheet The thought of having someone else in your home, even periodically, may be unsettling to many people, but it is not as bad as one thinks. Take time and make a list of rules and instructions. Include in that list, for example, to empty bathroom trash at the end of a shift. We have cats and do not want them outside, so I also included a note that they are to remain inside. Post this general information on a closet door or the bathroom door for easy reference by the caregiver. Depending upon the information included on your sheet, it can also provide the caregiver with a checklist until they get to know your parent better and get a routine down. It also helps when utilizing temporary help from an agency. Caregivers want to support your parent's schedule or the practices that you have initiated. They also might offer some very good alternatives from their experiences. Modify your information sheet as necessary.

Likes and Dislikes Take time to list foods that your parent likes and dislikes. Mom eats very small portions, and this list provides additional guidance on her preferences. Include in the information any special preferences, such as a glass of something cold to drink, followed by a cup of hot tea with half a packet of sweetener. Add this sheet to your notebook with the daily log sheets. Use tab dividers to separate sections. Make it known to each caregiver that this information is in the notebook, as they will welcome the reference when providing meals or snacks to your parent until they are familiar with his or her preferences.

Pay Record This is a very simple form that both you and the caregiver can use to keep track of hours worked, paydays, and payments. In the first column, indicate the week ending date. Some people prefer to end their weeks on Friday while others prefer Saturday or Sunday. At the end of each shift, make sure the hours are filled in for the caregiver(s) who worked that day. Total up the hours at the end of the week. There is space to record your check number and the amount paid. I also use a highlighter and draw through the entire week once I have issued payment. This will be a good check and balance for all parties.

Calendar I recommend inserting a calendar into one of the sections of your log book. Various stores should have calendars that are three-hole-punched, or you could punch holes in your favorite themed calendar. You can also retrieve monthly calendars through various links on the web to download and print. I find keeping this calendar in the log book helps organize doctors' appointments and tracking other pertinent information. This calendar also serves as a good record when doing your taxes, since mileage to doctors, hospitals, pharmacies, and other health-related travel may benefit your tax deductions.

Medications From your parent's prescribing physician(s) learn all the specifics of your parent's medication regime. Then it may be beneficial to seek out a mail-order prescription drug company for those ongoing, long-term maintenance drugs. Most insurance companies have an affiliate mail-order company that can be utilized. Your parent's physician(s) will be very accommodating in providing a ninety-day prescription to be sent in to the mail-order drug company. When a new prescription is to be administered and it is one that will be ongoing, always request two prescriptions; one to fill locally to begin dosing and one to be sent to the mail-order drug company. Doctors understand this routine and will be accommodating. Once established with the mail-order prescription drug company, it will be easy to reorder and minimize the possibility of running out of medications. Also, most insurers will offer reduced co-pays when ordering larger quantities.

We stumbled on a very easy way to dispense Mom's medications. This is especially important if you have outside help, as they will expect you to set aside the medications they are to give your parent during their shifts. We found it cumbersome to count out the pills each time medications were due or prior to leaving when the caregiver arrived. Forget those plastic pill holders that have dividers for each day of the week. They don't work for this purpose either.

One night while at a local establishment, we had an epiphany after receiving some sour cream in a small plastic container. We tipped the waitress extra, and she brought us a small bag with about seven of the containers and lids. I tried using color-coded dots with the time to be dispensed affixed to the tops of the containers, but those kept falling off. So, within the next few days, we ate at two other restaurants that had similar but different containers. I only needed three different types.

Each week I count out Mom's pills and sort them per container per time of day. I keep all her original medication bottles/packs in a plastic container. I then keep those I have put together in the small containers on a two-tiered tray near the notebook containing her daily log sheets and information. These are kept at one end of the kitchen counter, easily accessible by all of us. The aides love the idea, and it alleviates the problem of forgetting to set the meds aside for them to administer. It also makes medication dispensing easier for us too, since all we have to do is pick up the appropriate container at the appropriate time to give to Mom.

In most states, there are laws governing who can administer medications. Typically the caregiver can provide the medications for your parent to reach and self-administer. Check into the laws of your state and understand the limitations.

Chapter 9:
A Healing Rite of Passage

My journey to this place and time has been strained, as I'm sure you have deduced from your reading. However, for me too this has been a journey of personal healing. Reflecting back on the many emotional upheavals and the added stress of the known and unknown, I can honestly say I have successfully met my challenges head on and now view my previous struggles with my mother through different eyes. Taking a step back (and a deep breath) when making conscientious choices makes the difference between remaining unchanged in your current emotional state or solidifying your peace of mind and setting free your own internal demons—it did for me.

It is easy to use the excuses "We never got along" or "You don't understand." But I do understand. I too used these phrases because Mom and I didn't get along. I didn't think most people could grasp my strained relationship with my mother. We could never go shopping together. We couldn't do most anything that many adult mothers and daughters would do together.

My interactions with my mother since my father passed away always involved lists of things to do. She always had a job jar, and she expected me to do her bidding. I recall on one occasion that Mom, in a panic on the phone, insisted we come to Ohio. She said it was quite urgent but wouldn't go into details. I made immediate arrangements to leave work, and we flew to Ohio. When we arrived, she was on the front porch, looking aggravated. When I asked what was wrong, she pointed to the flower beds out front and insisted we pull the weeds. Once inside, she gave us a legal-size piece of paper listing a myriad of things to do, including moving items to the basement, changing curtains, and cleaning the gutters. We cleared almost everything on her list, but Larry drew the line at cleaning the gutters on a two-story house at our age. I did not mince words with Mom. I proceeded to tell her that just once I would like to make the trip to visit her without being greeted with a list of tasks and also that her list certainly did not warrant any urgency. I remember saying that I would no longer take time out from work to fly to Ohio to perform chores that she could hire someone to complete. Her only other option was to move to Florida. And her task lists? They only represented her unrealistic expectations!

My mother even tried to ground me on one occasion when I was forty years old! My son had spent a couple of weeks in the summer with my parents, and I had flown to Ohio to spend a few days and bring him back home. I wanted to use one of their two cars to go to the mall and visit some friends. Mom and Dad took afternoon naps, yet Mom just couldn't understand why my son and I thought we had to go running around while they were napping. I spent thirty-some years of my life in that town; I worked as an adult in that town; yet in her eyes, I had no business going to visit friends—I was there to see her and my Dad. A major conflagration followed. I rented a car and changed our flights, and my son and I flew home that night. I've had so many other similar incidents involving her through the years, but the time came to let go, to move on, and to heal.

I was under my mother's thumb while growing up, but after becoming an adult, I moved on. However, Mom has always tried to control aspects of my life and would have done so had I not been so stubborn and independent. To this day, now that I am fifty-six, she tries to continue the same relationship that we had when I was fifteen. I have chosen not to allow that to happen.

While wrestling with my own internal demons, I reflected on a story Larry told me about his youngest sister Mary. Larry is one of ten children. The stress and strain their parents experienced raising that many children and maintaining a farm in Ohio took its toll. Their parents split while some of the siblings were young, and the younger ones never really knew the nurturing side of their mother. Mary had always suffered a very strained relationship with their mother, too. She was raising (and home-schooling) three boys of her own. One day in conversation many years ago with Larry, she expressed the exhaustion she was experiencing in her own life while raising the three boys, and Larry told her to add seven more children to her three and she would begin to understand what happened to their mother. Mary, being the gentle spirit she was and is, realized that her mother wasn't able to give emotionally what she didn't have. Their mother at that time was suffering with the onset of Alzheimer's disease and was in a nursing facility. Mary discussed matters with her husband, and they moved her mother in to live with them. She lived in their home for thirteen years until her passing several years ago.

Mary's description of her whole experience and her emotional healing remained in my thoughts. She had a very rocky relationship with her mother, but she took the higher road and did what she believed was right. She had the courage to face her demons and the courage to tackle the challenge of parenting her parent. Mary says that even though she provided her mother a safe and secure environment, she benefited from the arrangement too. To this day, I sometimes seek out Mary for her encouragement and wisdom when dealing with the challenges that I currently face.

By acknowledging and understanding life's inevitable course, I could make the rational decisions that had to be made, decisions I would need to continue to make each and every day. I am able to view my mom's behavior through different eyes now, and I have found true peace within myself.

In poker there's the saying that "scared money doesn't win." I apply that concept to life and urge others to challenge themselves and not be afraid to confront whatever animosities might be lingering in their relationships with their parent(s), or with anyone for that matter. The journey, although stressful, will be a time of awareness, growth, and catharsis, as it has been for me.

You see, it's not what you have in life that matters, but what you do with it. I had the ability to give Mom safety and security and to enable her to enjoy some of the little things that made her happy. Who doesn't deserve that in their final days? I am very glad I have taken this journey and very glad Mom is able to enjoy her butter pecan ice cream, pecans, corn fritters, potato pancakes, chicken soup, pork chops, Pyrohi, and Hulushki that she so loves.

Not everyone has a loving relationship with his or her parents. Not everyone's story is like mine. But at the end of the day, if you undertake this voyage of healing, you will make positive changes and become a better person.

Remember that old saying, "Do unto others as you would want them to do unto you." Teach your children well so that someday they will be there to help you.

Chapter 10:
On Your Way

When dealing with elderly parents, especially when dementia is present, routines can minimize their frustration and yours. Keep in mind though, that at any time your parent may forget the routine, and that's okay. Routine just provides them some familiarity that makes them feel safe. Having a routine will benefit you, your family, and anyone else involved in their care by making daily activities less chaotic. Keep in mind that as an aging person's condition progresses, change can send that person into a tailspin at any time. Understanding this sensitivity to change will help you rationally confront a situation should it occur.

As costs continue to rise, services continue to decrease, and concerns continue to appear about various health issues characteristic of hospitals and facilities for the elderly, such as assisted living and nursing homes, more families are choosing to care for their loved ones within their own homes. Although home care may seem overwhelming at first, within no time at all the initial shock of your newly acquired responsibilities will subside. I hope that the suggestions contained herein will minimize the stress of everyday activities.

Understanding how scary diminishing capabilities are to your parent will assist you in managing any issues that may arise. Having a good support staff of doctors will offer some comfort when dealing with any problems, too. Based upon your parent's medical needs, a general practitioner may be enough. However, it may be necessary to establish your parent as a patient with a neurologist, a cardiologist, and an endocrinologist if your parent does not already utilize these specialists. Making good decisions while your parents are healthier and having a baseline to refer to in the future will prove beneficial as time passes.

At age fifty-six, I have collided head-on with the reality that I'm not as invincible as I once thought I was. Getting old is certainly not a picnic, and it seems like the older we get, the faster time flies. I hope that my experiences and actions will shed some light and encourage compassion in those whose lives I touch. Reflecting upon the past few years, Larry and I have learned to embrace moments of humor that continue to nourish the strength we need to cope with situations as they erupt.

Your story may be different from mine, but I guarantee that when dealing with aging parents, you will identify with the similarities. Please know that you are not alone. I look back over the past several years and all that has transpired. I try to keep in mind the fifty-two years Mom and Dad spent as husband and wife, being each other's daily companion. They loved dancing, camping, working in the yard, and so many other things. They lived a good life and cherished their time together on this earth.

Larry, with his usual sensitivity, has reminded me that many of the ways that my mother acted and responded during her time of declining health were due to no other reason than her normal human desire for autonomy and pleasure. I think of her brave red dancing dress. She just wanted to dance again!

So many times we are blinded by the overwhelming chain of events that we fail to see the simple answer right in front of us. Step back. Find the underlying motivation. It may shed light on situations, actions, and reactions. Remember, as we age, we tend to revert back to childish ways. Hence some of us find ourselves parenting our parents.

Appendix A:

Examples

General Instructions
(EXAMPLE)

General:

- CATS ARE INDOOR CATS. NEVER LEAVE DOORS OPEN. SEE THAT THEY DO NOT RUN OUT. As a rule, this issue should not be a problem.

- Always make sure there is a pad underneath Mom when she sits on the furniture. Pads are on the top shelf in bedroom closet.

- Most supplies needed are in the hall closet, under the sink, above the toilet, or in her bedroom.

- When she is sitting, please see that she does not lean her head to the side while napping. This position will cause her to have head, neck, and arm pain.

- When she is in bed, make sure she is high enough on her mattress that she can extend her legs freely; she should lie squarely on her back. Remind her to sleep on her back and not her side. See that her left arm is not caught under her; she has trouble moving it.

- When she becomes soiled, please make sure to clean her skin well before re-dressing. Her skin disorder becomes very aggravated if her skin is not thoroughly cleaned.

- Please complete the log sheet after giving her food, drinks, or meds.

- Empty her trash cans daily. The garbage can is in garage just through laundry room door. If the garbage can is not in the garage, put her bagged trash on the garage floor. PLEASE WATCH THAT THE CATS DO NOT GO OUT THE DOOR.

Eating:

- She is not on a special diet. Please encourage eating, especially when giving pills, to ensure that her stomach does not get upset. In the morning, she takes the antacid and fiber chew first, eats, and then takes the rest of her pills when she is nearly finished with her food. Monitor pills being taken, as she sometimes will drop them and not realize it. She will let you drop all the small ones in her mouth at once. Larger ones need to be taken individually.

Bathing:

- Use epsom salts in water. Epsom salts are stored in closet.

- Put white or pink rubber shoes on to prevent slipping.
- She may sit and enjoy the hydrotherapy for five to ten minutes before you wash her.
- She likes a wet towel (face towel size) placed on her back and one on her front while she is sitting in the tub.
- Once she is dry, please use anti-itch lotion over her body for the itching.
- Once her pull-ups are on, sprinkle some medicated powder at the waistline under her pull-ups (side to back to side).
- Wipe down the tub with cleanser from under the kitchen sink.
- There is spray deodorant to put on her. It is stored behind the toilet.

Dressing for bed:
- She requires one regular pull-up with a pad put in it. The pads are under the sink.
- She also requires a second pull-up (extra absorbency) from under the sink as the outer pull-up.
- She needs to brush her teeth.
- If not bathing that night, she likes a face wipe (on sink counter) to wipe her face with (needs water).
- She generally sits in the living room until 10:00 PM and then retires to bed to watch TV for one hour. Please use the sleep timer setting on the TV.
- Always make sure there is a pad on the bed before she retires to bed.

Likes and Dislikes
(EXAMPLE)

♦ **No diet restrictions.**
♦ **Keep portions small.**

Examples:
Smaller bowls for soup. Serving should be ⅓ to ½ cup.
Meat, about 2 oz. or less, has to be cut up for her.

Loves corn; can eat corn on the cob (buttered); will eat ½ to 1 full ear (broken in half). Corn skewers are in drawer next to stove on right. Corn can be cooked two minutes in microwave; do not put skewers in microwave.

Likes chicken broth. You can heat broth up on stove and swirl an egg white in the broth, then cook a minute or so longer.

When preparing her protein shake, you can add ½ to 1 teaspoon of flavored syrup to the protein drink. You can also add fresh fruit or ice cream to her protein shake. She loves butter pecan ice cream in it.

Likes

Apple slices, about ¼ apple	Sliced peaches
Apple sauce with cinnamon sprinkled on	Pecans—5-6 at a time in a bowl
Cantaloupe, about ½ cup cut up	Watermelon—about 1 cup
Cookies, 2 small	Strawberries, peaches, blueberries
Pecan rolls	Glazed doughnut holes
Corn fritters with butter (loves)	Pickles
Corn dogs (cut up)	Fish sticks
Chicken, pork, fish, roast beef, bacon	BBQ pork
Chicken-based soups—mostly broth	Potato pancakes with butter
Most Chinese food	Spaghetti
Mexican cheese, salsa with chips	Tortilla chips - nachos
French toast with butter	Scrambled eggs with cheese
Pizza	Cottage cheese
Cabbage	Tomatoes
Salad	Potatoes
Corn on the cob, creamed corn, corn soup	Waffles
Green peppers	Rice pudding

Root beer floats made with butter pecan ice cream	White bread toasted w/ margarine only
Onion rings	

Dislikes

Yogurt
Rice
Green beans, broccoli, peas, lima beans

Daily Log Sheet
Name: _____ Day/Date: _____

(Time) When indicating foods try to estimate ounces, cups, etc.

Breakfast 8:00 AM	1/3 c oatmeal w/soymilk 6 oz hot tea 4 oz cranberry juice	8 oz. protein drink w/raspberry flavoring 4 oz water
Lunch 11:30 AM	2 fish sticks ¼ c applesauce 2 onion rings ⅓ cup fruit salad	4 oz. diet soda 6 oz water
Dinner 5:00 PM	½ c chicken broth ½ ear corn 2 oz baked chicken w/rice 1 pc. banana bread	6 oz hot tea 4 oz water 2 oz prune juice
Snacks 2:00 PM 8:00 PM	¼ apple, sliced, and 4 pecans; 4 oz diet soda 5 corn chips with salsa; 6 oz hot tea; 4 oz diet soda	

MEDICATIONS   TIME

Medicine Name Prescribed Dosage	Orders Frequency	Doctor's Name Date Prescribed	AM	AM	PM	PM	PM	PM
Drug Name/Dosage	1 tab 2x per day	Dr. Smith 4-19-08	8:00					8:00
Drug Name/Dosage	1 tab 2X per day	Dr. Smith 4-19-08	8:00					8:00
Drug Name/Dosage	2 tabs 2x per day	Dr. Smith 4-19-08	8:00			2:00		8:00
Drug Name/Dosage	1 daily	Dr. Jones 5-10-08	8:00					
Drug Name/Dosage	1 daily	Dr. Smith 4-19-08						8:00
Drug Name/Dosage	2x daily		8:00	12:00				
Drug Name/Dosage	2x daily	Dr. ABC 6-12-08	8:00				4:00	
Drug Name/Dosage	1 daily				2:00			
Drug Name/Dosage PRN								
Drug Name/Dosage PRN								
Multivitamin/dosage	1 daily		8:00					

BLOOD PRESSURE – PULSE – TEMPERATURE (as necessary)

Time	Readings	Notes
3:00 PM	BP=136/72 P=65	

DAILY NOTES

AM-BM - normal Therapy in PM Bath

Appendix B:

Forms

Doctor's Information Form

Name _____   **DOB:** _____

CURRENT MEDICATIONS AS OF _____

MEDICATIONS   TIME

Medicine Name Prescribed Dosage	Orders- Frequency	Doctor's Name Date Prescribed	AM	PM	PM	PM	PM
LIST ITEMS THAT ARE TAKEN AS NEEDED (PRN) BELOW THIS LINE							

Notes: _____
_____
_____
_____
_____

Questions: _____
_____
_____
_____
_____
_____
_____
_____

Medical Information Form

Name: _____   **Date:** _____

Provide general information: (check all that apply)

○ DO NOT RESUSCITATE (DNR) executed

○ Durable Power of Attorney and Power Attorney for Health Care executed

○ Living Will executed

Authorized Persons
Authorized to talk to the following regarding condition including her physicians (provide names, phone numbers and relationship):

Personal Information

Address	City, state and Zip code	Phone

Social Security Number		Date of Birth
Emergency Contact	(Name, Relationship, & Phone Numbers)	
Alternate Emergency Contact	(Name, Relationship, & Phone Numbers)	
Insurance	(Company & Policy Number)	

Allergies

Medical Conditions

Medical Restrictions

Medical Information Form

Name:_____   **Date:** _____

Hospitalizations

Condition/Diagnosis	When	Where

Physicians, Labs, Medical Service Providers

Type	Name	Address	Phone (Incl. Area Code)
General			
Cardiologist			
Neurologist			
Endocrinologist			
Podiatrist			
Dentist			
Optometrist			
Psychologist/Psychiatrist			
Chiropractor			

Signed _____
Identify if Power of Attorney

Print Name _____

Daily Log Sheet

Name: _____   Day/Date: _____

(Time)   When indicating foods, try to estimate ounces, cups, etc.

Breakfast	
Lunch	
Dinner	
Snacks	

MEDICATIONS   TIME

Medicine Name Prescribed Dosage	Orders-Frequency	Doctor's Name Date Prescribed	AM	AM	PM	PM	PM	PM
INDICATE MEDICATIONS TAKEN AS NEEDED (PRN) BELOW THIS LINE								

BLOOD PRESSURE – PULSE – TEMPERATURE (as necessary)

Time	Readings	Notes

DAILY NOTES

Pay Record

Name: _____   Year _____

Date Wk Beginning	Sun	Mon	Tues	Wed	Thurs	Fri	Sat	Total Hrs.	Paid
MONTH:									
MONTH:									

Personal Notes

Personal Notes

Personal Notes